JOHN F. KENNEDY
1917—1963

Chronology - Documents - Bibliographical Aids

Edited by
Ralph A. Stone

Series Editor
Howard F. Bremer

1971
OCEANA PUBLICATIONS, INC.
Dobbs Ferry, New York

Library of Congress Catalog Card Number: 75-116063
International Standard Book Number: 0-379-12076-3

Manufactured in the United States of America

CONTENTS

CONTENTS

Editor's Foreword

EDITOR'S FOREWORD

John F. Kennedy was President for only slightly more than a thousand days. His tragically shortened term of office will make future historical evaluations of his record difficult. At the moment it would appear that he will receive at least moderate credit and perhaps even high praise, if not for his actual accomplishments, for what he attempted and represented. He was a young man — 43 years old — the youngest ever to be elected President, who symbolized for many the youthfulness and vigor which the country badly needed. He possessed a keen sense of humor which helped relieve the grimness of the crises he faced as President. His program "to get America moving again" was ambitious. Most of his proposals had not been enacted before his assassination. They had been put forward, however, and eloquently so. Kennedy's prose was seldom lifeless, and the reader who wishes to pursue his study of Kennedy can do no better than to turn to his own words.

The purpose of this slim volume is to outline the important events in John F. Kennedy's life, provide a sampling of his most important addresses, and suggest works by and about the man and his time.

CHRONOLOGY

CHRONOLOGY

EARLY LIFE

1917

May 29   Born in Brookline, Massachusetts, the second of what would eventually be a family of nine children. His father, Joseph P. Kennedy, banker, financier, diplomat; his mother, Rose Fitzgerald.

1917-1926

Lived at 83 Beals Street in Brookline. Attended the Dexter school there.

1925

November 20   Robert F. Kennedy, brother, born.

1926

Family moved to New York City, where they lived at 252nd Street and Independence Avenue, Riverdale-on-Hudson. John ("Jack") Kennedy attended fourth, fifth, and sixth grades at the Riverdale Country Day School.

1929

Family moved to Bronxville, New York, and Joseph Kennedy bought what became the main house in the Kennedy compound at Hyannis Port, Massachusetts.

1930

Spent one year in a Catholic prepartory school, Canterbury, at New Milford, Massachusetts.

1931

At the age of fourteen, he enrolled at Choate, a private school at Wallingford, Connecticut.

1932

February 22   Edward M. Kennedy, brother, born.

1

1935
Graduated from Choate, 64th in a class of 112. He went to England that summer to study at the London School of Economics, but returned prematurely to the United States because of an attack of jaundice.

Fall   Entered Princeton University but dropped out in December after a recurrence of jaundice.

1936
Fall   Entered Harvard. Tried out for several sports which excited him much more than academic subjects. He was moderately active in extracurricular affairs, winning a position on the Crimson, the undergraduate daily newspaper. Showed little interest in politics.

1937
Summer   Toured Europe with a close friend from Choate. Visited France, Spain, and Italy, where he had an audience with the Pope. Upon his return to Harvard he became more interested in his studies, particularly international relations.

December   Joseph P. Kennedy appointed Ambassador to Britain by President Roosevelt.

1938
May 29   At the age of 21 John F. Kennedy received a $1 million trust fund established by his father.

1939
The second semester of his Junior year at Harvard was spent in Europe, travelling in Poland, Russia, Turkey, Germany, and France. He also worked briefly in his father's Embassy office in London.

1940
June 21   Graduated from Harvard cum laude with a Bachelor of Science degree. To obtain honors in his major field of study, political science, he wrote an undergraduate thesis, entitled "Appeasement in Europe."

July   His honors' thesis was published as <u>Why England Slept</u> (New York, Wilfred Funk, Inc.), a critical analysis of Britain's apathy and lack of military preparedness before World War II. The book received praise from reviewers and also became a best-seller.

Fall   Enrolled at Stanford University for graduate study in business. Quit school after six months.

                              1941
February   Left Stanford to travel throughout South America.

                     THE NAVY IN WORLD WAR II

September   Enlisted in the Navy.

                              1943
March   Given command of PT-109. He held the rank of Lieutenant (j.g.).

August 2   His torpedo boat was rammed by Japanese destroyer in the South Pacific. For heroism in rescuing an injured man and leading his crew to safety, was awarded the Purple Heart and Navy and Marine Corps Medal.

December   Because of malaria and a recurring back injury, he was sent back to the United States.

                              1944
August 12   His brother, Joseph Kennedy, Jr., the oldest son in the family, killed while piloting an airplane over Europe.

                              1945
April   Honorably discharged from the Navy.

June   As a special correspondent for the New York <u>Journal American</u>, he covered the San Francisco conference

founding the United Nations. Ended his journalistic
career after reporting on the British elections from
London that same summer.

CONGRESSMAN

1946

June   Entered upon his political career by winning the Dem-
                        ocratic nomination for Congressman from Massachu-
                        setts' Eleventh District.

November 5   Elected Congressman.

1947

January   At the age of 29, took his seat in the House of Repre-
                        sentatives, where he served 3 terms.

June 4   One of 79 Congressmen to vote against the Taft-Hartley
                        Bill. He generally favored President Truman's do-
                        mestic policies in the areas of social-welfare, pro-
                        gressive taxation, and business regulation. On econ-
                        omy and efficiency in government, he tended to be
                        more conservative; on civil liberties, ambivalent.

1949

January 25   In speech in Congress attacked Truman's foreign pol-
                        icy for having let China "fall" to Communists.

February   Berated the Administration for inadequate military
                        defense spending.

SENATOR

1952

April   Announced his decision to seek the Senate seat held
                        by Henry Cabot Lodge, Jr. Began intensive campaign,
                        ably assisted by his brothers, sisters, and parents.

November 4   Defeated Lodge to become U.S. Senator from Massa-
                    chusetts. Dwight D. Eisenhower elected President.

                                   1953
July 31   Brother, Robert, resigned as lawyer-investigator for
                    Joseph McCarthy's Senate subcommittee. The usual
                    liberal record of both Kennedys was later hurt by this
                    connection with the controversial McCarthy.

September 12   Married Jacqueline Bouvier.

                                   1954
October 21   Entered Manhattan Hospital for back operation.

                                   1955
February   Underwent a second back operation. While convales-
                    cing, wrote Profiles in Courage, brief biographies of
                    courageous American politicians. The book was pub-
                    lished in 1956 and won the Pulitzer Prize for Biography
                    in 1957.

                                   1956
August   Nominated Adlai Stevenson for President at Demo-
                    cratic national convention. Lost to Estes Kefauver in
                    his bid for the Vice Presidential nomination.

                                   1957
November 27   Birth of a daughter, Caroline Bouvier Kennedy.

                                   1958
November 4   Reelected by nearly one million votes to a second
                    term as Senator.

                                   1960
January 2   Press conference: "I am announcing today my candi-
                    dacy for the Presidency of the United States."

April 5   Won primary in Wisconsin against Senator Hubert H.
                    Humphrey.

May 10	Humphrey withdrew from race after losing to Kennedy in West Virginia.
May 20	Won Oregon primary over Senator Wayne Morse.
July 13	In Los Angeles, received nomination for Presidency on first ballot. Lyndon B. Johnson of Texas nominated for Vice Presidency.
September 12	Speech in Houston facing Catholic issue: "Contrary to common newspaper usage, I am not the Catholic candidate for President. I am the Democratic party's candidate for President."
September 26	First of four televised debates with Richard M. Nixon, Republican candidate for President.
November 8	Elected 35th President of the United States by less than 119,000 votes out of a total of more than 68,000,000. The electoral vote was: Kennedy, 303; Nixon, 219; Senator Harry F. Byrd (Democrat, Virginia), 15. He was the youngest man and the first Catholic ever to be elected President.
November 9	Named Clark Clifford as his liaison with outgoing administration.
November 14	Met with Vice President Nixon at Key Biscayne, Florida.
November 17	Briefed on CIA involvement in training Cuban exiles in Guatemala to invade Cuba and overthrow Castro.
November 25	Birth of a son, John F. Kennedy, Jr.

PRESIDENT

1961

January 19	Last meeting with President Eisenhower, with much discussion on Southeast Asia and Cuba.

January 20   Inaugurated. First American President born in the twentieth century.

January 21   Cabinet appointees: State Department, Dean Rusk; Treasury, C. Douglas Dillon; Defense, Robert S. McNamara; Attorney General, Robert F. Kennedy; Postmaster General, J. Edward Day (replaced by John A. Gronouski, September 30, 1963); Interior, Stewart L. Udall; Agriculture, Orville Freeman; Commerce, Luther Hodges; Labor, Arthur J. Goldberg (replaced by W. Willard Wirtz, August 31, 1962); Health, Education and Welfare, Abraham Ribicoff (replaced by Anthony J. Celebrezze, July 31, 1962).

Presidential Staff appointees: David Bell, Budget Director; McGeorge Bundy, Special Assistant for National Security Affairs; Richard Goodwin, Assistant Special Counsel to the President; Lawrence O'Brien, Special Assistant for Legislative Liaison; Kenneth O'Donnell, Appointments Secretary; Pierre Salinger, Press Secretary; Arthur Schlesinger, Jr., Special Assistant on Latin American Affairs; Theodore Sorensen, Special Counsel to the President; Walt M. Rostow, Deputy Special Assistant to the President for National Security; Jerome B. Wiesmer, Science Advisor; Walter Heller, head of the Council of Economic Advisors; Ralph Dungan, Special Assistant in charge of personnel.

Other key appointments: Chester A. Bowles, Under Secretary of State; George W. Ball, Under Secretary for Economic Affairs; Robert V. Roosa, Under Secretary for Monetary Affairs; H. H. Fowler, Under Secretary of the Treasury; Adolf A. Berle, Jr., special advisor on Latin American affairs and chairman of the Latin American Task Force; Edward R. Murrow, head of the United States Information Agency; Newton N. Minow, chairman of the Federal Communications

Commission; Averell Harriman, Ambassador at Large; Adlai Stevenson, Ambassador to the United Nations; George McGovern, director of the Food for Peace Program; Thomas K. Finletter, United States representative to NATO; Glenn T. Seaborg, chairman of the Atomic Energy Commission; James E. Webb, head of the National Aeronautics and Space Administration.

January 22	Allen Dulles of the CIA briefed key cabinet members on plans to use Cuban exiles to overthrow Castro.
January 30	Delivered first State of the Union message, stressing dangers abroad and economic problems at home.
February 2	Special message to Congress; program for economic recovery and growth.
February 6	Special message to Congress on gold and the balance of payments deficit.
February 7	Asked Congress to raise Minimum Wage from $1 to $1.25 and extend coverage to over 4 million more workers.
February 9	Requested legislation assisting medical and dental colleges and universities.
February 10	Appointed Henry A. Kissinger consultant on national security problems.
February 20	Special message to Congress asked for a package of $5,625 billion for federal aid for education.
March 1	Peace Corps created by executive order. Brother-in-law Sargent Shriver named its director, with Bill D. Moyers and Richard Goodwin as top aides.
March 13	Alliance for Progress announced at a White House reception for members of Congress and for the diplomatic corps of the Latin American republics.

onfer with

ig-term foreign aid program with em-
-help.

ceasefire must precede negotiations
nd independent Laos.

n London.

esentatives narrowly voted against a
l Security   um wage bill, supporting a substitute
). Carl Albert of Oklahoma led fight
measure.

Kennedy's

initiation of program to rapidly in-
strength.

halt water

ace, Soviet Major Yuri Gagarin, or-

ican people
Presidency   sion of Cuba.
intry faced
, nor could   iet Premier Khrushchev concerning
dens of this
those bur-
neet Soviet   x-President Eisenhower on Cuba at
ryland. Held joint press conference.

tional sea-   "Freedom riders"--boarded south-
challenge segregation in interstate

velopment Act.

eat in Con-   S. astronaut, Alan Shepard.
st domestic
mum wage bill covering 3,624,000
s.

va, Canada.

wly created   osed a space effort designed to put
ID).   team on the moon in this decade.

May 31   Along with Mrs. Kennedy, flew to Paris to c
                    President Charles de Gaulle.

June 3-4   Met with Premier Khrushchev in Vienna.

June 4-5   Conferred with Prime Minister MacMillan

June 30   Signed Housing Act and bill extending Soci
                    benefits.

July 7   Adolf A. Berle, Jr. resigned as chairman o
                    task force on Latin America.

July 20   Signed a bill doubling federal effort to
                    pollution.

July 25   Radio and television report to the Amer
                    on the Berlin crisis: "When I ran for the
                    of the United States, I knew that this co
                    serious challenges, but I could not realize
                    any man realize who does not bear the bur
                    office, how heavy and constant would be
                    dens ...." Called for $3.5 billion to
                    pressures.

August 7   Signed the first of three bills creating n
                    shore parks.

August 13   Erection of Berlin Wall by East German

August 20   United States troops sent to West Berlin

                    The President's education bill suffered de
                    gress, Kennedy perhaps meeting his wor
                    setback.

September 3   Signed the $1.25 Minimum Wage Bill.

September 20   Named Fowler Hamilton head of a ne
                    Agency for International Development (

September 22   Signed bill establishing federal program to help com-
                  bat juvenile delinquency.

September 26   Signed bill establishing the first full-scale, full-time
                  disarmament agency. Named W. C. Foster its director.

October 24   Peace Corps and fiscal policy scored by General
                  Eisenhower.

December 15   Renewed American commitment to preserve indepen-
                  dence of the Republic of Vietnam and pledged assist-
                  ance to its defense effort.

December 15-17   With Mrs. Kennedy received enthusiastic receptions
                  on trip to Puerto Rico, Venezuela and Colombia.

                                    1962
January 11   In annual State of the Union message asked for author-
                  ity to reduce tariffs, and if necessary, to reduce in-
                  come taxes.

January 24   At news conference announced intention to create a
                  Department of Urban Affairs by executive order, and
                  stated that Robert C. Weaver would be its head.

February 3   Announced a near total embargo on trade with Cuba.

February 7   Special message to Congress proposed creation of a
                  privately owned corporation for the communications
                  satellite system.

February 8   Established a United States Military Command in
                  South Vietnam commanded by General Paul D. Haskins.
                  About 4,000 Americans acted as advisors and partici-
                  pated in air support.

February 20   First United States orbital flight by John H. Glenn.

January 21   House rejected, 264-150, the President's plan for a
                  cabinet department of urban affairs and housing.

March 12-26   Mrs. Kennedy visited Pakistan and India on good will
                  tour.

March 18   Message to Chairman Khrushchev proposing joint
                  action in the exploration of outer space.

April 5   Called for overhaul of federal transportation policy,
                  and renewed request for urban mass transportation
                  program.

April 11   Denounced U.S. Steel's raising of prices as wholly
                  unjustifiable and an irresponsible defiance of the
                  public interest.

April 13   Steel price rise rescinded.

April 16   Appointed Byron R. White Associate Justice of the
                  Supreme Court.

May 15   Sent troops to Thailand to assume positions on the
                  Laotian border.

May 20   Spoke at Medicare rally in Madison Square Garden.

June 29-July 1   State visit to Mexico with Mrs. Kennedy. Received
                  by President Lopez Mateos and an enthusiastic Mexi-
                  can people.

July 26   Signed bill providing for revision of public welfare
                  laws, emphasizing family rehabilitation and train-
                  ing instead of dependency.

August 8-31   Mrs. Kennedy vacationed in Italy accompanied by
                  Caroline.

August 30	Named W. Willard Wirtz Secretary of Labor to succeed Arthur Goldberg.
Sept. 30-Oct. 1	Segregationists staged fifteen-hour riot on University of Mississippi campus, protesting admission of black applicant, James Merideth, into the university. Two persons killed, many injured. Federal troops and marshals ordered in by the President to insure Meredith's admission and preserve order.
October 1	Appointed Arthur J. Goldberg Associate Justice of the Supreme Court.
October 2	Signed United Nations Bond Bill authorizing American participation in financing United Nations peace-keeping operations in Congo and elsewhere.
October 10	Signed first major improvement in Food and Drug laws since 1938, protecting families against untested and ineffective drugs.
October 11	Signed Trade Expansion Act granting President unprecedented authority to reduce or eliminate tariffs.
October 16-28	Cuban missile crisis and blockade.
October 22	Announced imposition of "quarantine" on Cuba because of construction by Russians of offensive missile bases.
October 28	Soviet Premier Khrushchev agreed to halt construction of missile bases in Cuba and to remove Soviet rockets under United Nations supervision.
November 6	Brother Edward M. Kennedy won balance of term for Senate seat from Massachusetts vacated by John by defeating Republican Henry Cabot Lodge. He won a six year term in 1964.

November 10   With Mrs. Kennedy attended funeral of Eleanor Roosevelt at Hyde Park. The widow of President Franklin
D. Roosevelt had died in New York City November 7.

November 20   Announced the lifting of the naval blockade of Cuba.
Signed executive order to prevent racial discrimi-
nation in federal housing.

November 28   Named Budget Director David E. Bell to succeed Fowler
Hamilton as foreign aid director (AID). Appointed
Kermit Gorden to succeed Bell.

November 29   Fund-raising dinner for the National Cultural Center
in Washington, D.C. (renamed, in 1964, the John F.
Kennedy Center for the Performing Arts).

December 29   With Mrs. Kennedy reviewed in Miami, Florida, the
Cuban invasion brigade which had been released by
a ransom agreement on December 23.

1963

January 14   Delivered his last State of the Union Address. Called
for tax cuts and tax reform.

January 17   Sent Congress the biggest budget so far, $98 billion
with a planned deficit of more than $10 billion.

January 20   Letters between Premier Khrushchev and the President on nuclear test-ban treaty were published.

February 1   Secretary of State Rusk announced that the President
had authorized resumption of underground nuclear
tests in Nevada.

February 14   Proposed a domestic Peace Corps.

February 21   Proposed a hospital insurance plan to be financed
through social security.

February 28	Sent civil rights message to Congress, with stress on Negro voting rights.
March 15	Signed a $435 million Manpower and Development Act.
March 19	Signed Declaration of Central America in San Jose, Costa Rica, pledging opposition to Soviet aggression in the Western Hemisphere with United States aid.
March 22	Urged final action on a Constitutional amendment outlawing poll tax as a bar to voting; it became the 24th Amendment.
March 29	Signed bill extending the Selective Service Act for four years. The Army announced that it expected to call up 90,000 men each year.
April 3	Told news conference that some 4,000 Soviet troops had left Cuba in March.
April 6	Named Chester Bowles ambassador to India.
April 19	Praised steel companies for acting with restraint in raising steel prices.
May 11	Issued joint communique with Canadian Prime Minister Lester Pearson from Hyannis Port stressing close relations between the two countries.
May 12	The President dispatched federal troops to bases near Birmingham, Alabama when race riots broke out there.
June 4	Signed bill changing the banking of $1 and $2 bills from silver to gold.
June 10	Speech at American University, Washington, D.C.: "I speak of peace as the necessary, rational end of rational man."

June 11   Mobilized Alabama National Guard to admit two black
                     students into University of Alabama as ordered by
                     court. In television report to the nation on civil rights:
                     "If an American, because his skin is dark, cannot
                     enjoy the full and free life that all of us want, then
                     who among us would be content to have the color of
                     his skin changed and stand in his place?"

June 19   Sent strong civil rights message to Congress urging
                     legislation to give all Americans equal opportunity
                     in education, employment, public accomodations,
                     voting, and access to federal programs.

June 20   Agreement for direct communication link with Soviet
                     Union ("hot line") reached at Geneva.

June 23-July 2   Trip to Germany, Ireland, England, Italy, conferring
                     with German Chancellor Adenauer, Vice Chancellor
                     Erhard, British Prime Minister Macmillan, Pope Paul
                     VI, Italian President Segni, et al.

June 26   Speech in West Berlin: "Two thousand years ago, the
                     proudest boast was, 'Civis Romanus sum.' Today in
                     the world of freedom, the proudest boast is, 'Ich bin
                     ein Berliner!'"

July 8   Ordered ban on almost all financial transactions with
                     Cuba in attempt to isolate Castro.

July 17   Senate defeated Kennedy's proposal for medical care
                     for the aged to be financed partly by Social Security.

July 18   Presented additional administrative proposals to sta-
                     bilize balance of payments and stem outflow of gold.

July 23   Called upon Congress to modify the nation's immigra-
                     tion laws, substituting for the national origins system
                     a policy recognizing skills of the immigrant regard-
                     less of place of birth.

July 25   A nuclear test-ban treaty in the atmosphere, space
                 and under water signed in Moscow by the United
                 States, Great Britain, and the Soviet Union.

July 26   Reported to the nation on the Nuclear Test Ban Treaty,
                 calling it a step toward peace but not necessarily a
                 preventive of war.

August 7   A son, Patrick Bouvier Kennedy, born. Died August 9.

August 21   Stressed the need of a tax reduction bill to stimulate
                 economy.

August 28   Civil rights march on Washington of some 200,000
                 persons, mostly black, to symbolize demands for
                 "Freedom--Now."

                 President's statement on civil rights march: "The
                 cause of 20 million Negroes has been advanced by the
                 program conducted so appropriately before the Na-
                 tion's shrine to the Great Emancipater, but even more
                 significant is the contribution to all mankind."

August 31   Signed bill creating a private corporation to operate
                 the communications satellite system.

September 2   Statement on Vietnam: "In the final analysis it is their
                 war. They are the ones who have to win it or lose
                 it. We can help them, ...but they have to win it, the
                 people of Vietnam, against the Communists."

September 20   Addressed United Nations General Assembly. Pro-
                 posed cooperation with Soviet Union, including outer
                 space exploration.

September 22   Nuclear test-ban treaty ratified by Senate, 80-19.

September 24-28   Visited eleven western states to encourage stronger conservation measures.

October 2   Signed bill loaning $100 million to the United Nations, if other nations made similar proportional loans.

October 9   At a press conference announced an agreement with Soviet Union to open private negotiations for sale of American wheat.

October 10   Signed bill controlling possibly hazardous drugs like thalidomide.

October 11   Remarks at presentation of the Final Report of the President's Commission on the Status of Women: "Women /should7 have the chance to use their powers, their full powers, intellectual powers, emotional powers, ... along the lines of excellence."

October 16   Signed bill providing minor tax reforms.

October 24   Signed Maternal and Child Health and Mental Retardation Bill.

October 26   Remarks at dedication of Robert Frost Library at Amherst, Massachusetts: "When power leads man towards arrogance, poetry reminds him of his limitations....When power corrupts, poetry cleanses."

November 1   President Ngo Dinh Diem and brother Ngo Dinh Nhu assassinated in Vietnam coup.

November 13   Instituted emergency assistance program for destitute areas of eastern Kentucky as part of permanent program of economic recovery for Appalachian region.

November 16   Obtained the release of Frederick Barghoorn, Yale professor who had been imprisoned in Russia on espionage charges.

November 21   Asked economic advisors to prepare "War on Poverty" program for 1964.

Delcared that almost all United States' tariffs were subject to reduction in 1964 under the General Agreement on Tariffs and Trade.

November 22   Shot by an assassin in Dallas, Texas and died at 1 P.M., C.S.T. The Governor of Texas, John Connally, was seriously wounded, but recovered. Vice President Johnson sworn in as 36th President in the presidential plane at Dallas.

November 24   Lee Harvey Oswald, accused assassin of President Kennedy, shot and killed by Jack Ruby (originally Rubenstein) while in custody of the Dallas police.

November 25   State funeral and burial with full military honors in Washington in the Arlington National Cemetery, attended by many foreign dignitaries including heads of states, and watched by millions of Americans over television.

DOCUMENTS

DOCUMENTS

will light our country and all who serve it — and the glow from
an truly light the world.

o, my fellow Americans: ask not what your country can d
ask what you can do for your country.

llow citizens of the world: ask not what America will do fo
what together we can do for the freedom of man.

ly, whether you are citizens of America or citizens of th
sk of us here the same high standards of strength and sacrifice
e ask of you. With a good conscience our only sure reward
ory the final judge of our deeds, let us go forth to lead the lan
, asking His blessing and His help, but knowing that here o
d's work must truly be our own.

DOCUMENTS

INAUGURAL ADDRESS
January 20, 1961

*The President spoke at 12:52 p.m. from a platform erec-
ted at the east front of the Capitol. No Kennedy speech
ever received more careful attention or underwent so
many drafts. It will undoubtedly remain the most quoted
of all his addresses.*

We observe today not a victory of party but a celebration of freedom — symbolizing an end as well as a beginning — signifying renewal
as well as change. For I have sworn before you and Almighty God the
same solemn oath our forebears prescribed nearly a century and
three quarters ago.

The world is very different now. For man holds in his mortal
hands the power to abolish all forms of human poverty and all forms
of human life. And yet the same revolutionary beliefs for which our
forebears fought are still at issue around the globe — the belief that
the rights of man come not from the generosity of the state but from
the hand of God.

We dare not forget today that we are the heirs of that first revolution. Let the word go forth from this time and place, to friend and foe
alike, that the torch has been passed to a new generation of Americans
— born in this century, tempered by war, disciplined by a hard and bitter peace, proud of our ancient heritage — and unwilling to witness or
permit the slow undoing of those human rights to which this nation
has always been committed, and to which we are committed today at
home and around the world.

Let every nation know, whether it wishes us well or ill, that we
shall pay any price, bear any burden, meet any hardship, support any
friend, oppose any foe to assure the survival and the success of liberty.

This much we pledge — and more.

To those old allies whose cultural and spiritual origins we share,
we pledge the loyalty of faithful friends. United, there is little we cannot do in a host of cooperative ventures. Divided, there is little we can

do — for we dare not meet a powerful challenge at odds and split asunder.

To those new states whom we welcome to the ranks of the free, we pledge our word that one form of colonial control shall not have passed away merely to be replaced by a far more iron tyranny. We shall not always expect to find them supporting our view. But we shall always hope to find them strongly supporting their own freedom — and to remember that, in the past, those who foolishly sought power by riding the back of the tiger ended up inside.

To those peoples in the huts and villages of half the globe struggling to break the bonds of mass misery, we pledge our best efforts to help them help themselves, for whatever period is required — not because the communists may be doing it, not becuase we seek their votes, but because it is right. If a free society cannot help the many who are poor, it cannot save the few who are rich.

To our sister republics south of our border, we offer a special pledge — to convert our good words into good deeds — in a new alliance for progress — to assist free men and free governments in casting off the chains of poverty. But this peaceful revolution of hope cannot become the prey of hostile powers. Let all our neighbors know that we shall join with them to oppose aggression or subversion anywhere in the Americas. And let every other power know that this Hemisphere intends to remain the master of its own house.

To that world assembly of sovereign states, the United Nations, our last best hope in an age where the instruments of war have far outpaced the instruments of peace, we renew our pledge of support — to prevent it from becoming merely a forum for invective — to strengthen its shield of the new and the weak — and to enlarge the area in which its writ may run.

Finally, to those nations who would make themselves our adversary, we offer not a pledge but a request: that both sides begin anew the quest for peace, before the dark powers of destruction unleashed by science engulf all humanity in planned or accidental self-destruction.

We dare not tempt them with weakness. For only when our arms are sufficient beyond doubt can we be certain beyond doubt that they will never be employed.

But neither can two great and powerful groups of nations take comfort from our present course — both sides overburdened by the cost of modern weapons, both rightly alarmed by the steady spread of the deadly atom, yet both racing to alter that uncertain balance of terror that stays the hand of mankind's final war.

So let us being anew — remembering on both sides that civility is not a sign of weakness, and sincerity is always subject to proof.

Let us never negotiate out of fear. But let us never fe[ar to negoti]ate.

Let both sides explore what problems unite us in[stead of lab]oring those problems which divide us.

Let both sides, for the first time, formulate se[rious and precise] proposals for the inspection and control of arms [— and bring the ab]solute power to destroy other nations under the ab[solute control of all] nations.

Let both sides seek to invoke the wonders o[f science instead of its] terrors. Together let us explore the stars, co[nquer the deserts, erad]icate disease, tap the ocean depths and enc[ourage the arts and com]merce.

Let both sides unite to heed in all co[rners of the earth the com]mand of Isaiah — to "undo the heavy [burdens ... and to let the op]pressed go free."

And if a beach-head of cooperati[on may push back the jungle of] suspicion, let both sides join in cre[ating a new endeavor, not a new] balance of power, but a new world [of law, where the strong are just] and the weak secure and the peace [preserved.]

All this will not be finished in [the first 100 days. Nor will] it be finished in the first one [thousand days, nor in the life of this] Administration, nor even perh[aps in our lifetime on this planet. But] let us begin.

In your hands, my fello[w citizens, more than mine, will rest the] final success or failure of [our course. Since this country was founded,] each generation of Ameri[cans has been summoned to give testimony] to its national loyalty. T[he graves of young Americans who answered] the call to service surr[ound the globe.]

Now the trumpet [summons us again — not as a call to bear arms, though] arms we ne[ed — not as a call to battle, though embattled we] are — but a call to [bear the burden of a long twilight struggle, year in] and year out, "re[joicing in hope, patient in tribulation" — a struggle] against the comm[on enemies of man: tyranny, poverty, disease and] war itself.

Can we for[ge against these enemies a grand and global alliance,] North and So[uth, East and West, that can assure a more fruitful life] for all mank[ind? Will you join in that historic effort?]

In the [long history of the world, only a few generations have been] granted [the role of defending freedom in its hour of maximum danger.] I do not [shrink from this responsibility — I welcome it. I do not believe] that ar[y of us would exchange places with any other people or any other] gener[ation.]

FIRST ANNUAL MESSAGE TO CONGRESS
January 30, 1961

Ten days after his inaugural the President presented to Congress the first of his reports on the State of the Union. Beginning on a somber note, he outlined the problems facing the nation. The economy was in the wake of a recession; there was a balance of payments gap; the cities were engulfed in squalor; classrooms were inadequate to meet the demand; conservation of natural resources had been neglected. Abroad, the outlook was even more perilous. The Communist "menace" was growing. The "free world" was in a state of disarray. Relations with the Soviet Union and Communist China remained uncertain. To meet these problems, Kennedy proposed a number of changes which he would spell out more fully in the coming months.

. . . I speak today in an hour of national peril and national opportunity. Before my term has ended, we shall have to test anew whether a nation organized and governed such as ours can endure. The outcome is by no means certain. The answers are by no means clear. All of us together — this Administration, this Congress, this nation — must forge those answers.

But today, were I to offer — after little more than a week in office — detailed legislation to remedy every national ill, the Congress would rightly wonder whether the desire for speed had replaced the duty of responsibility.

My remarks, therefore, will be limited. But they will also be candid. To state the facts frankly is not to despair the future nor indict the past. The prudent heir takes careful inventory of his legacies, and gives a faithful accounting to those whom he owes an obligation of turst. And, while the occasion does not call for another recital of our blessings and assets, we do have no greater asset than the willingness of a free and determined people, through its elected officials, to face all problems frankly and meet all dangers free from panic or fear.

I.

The present state of our economy is disturbing. We take office in the wake of seven months of recession, three and one-half years of slack, seven years of diminished economic growth, and nine years of falling farm income.

Business bankruptcies have reached their highest level since the Great Depression. Since 1951 farm income has been squeezed down by 25 percent. Save for a brief period in 1958, insured unemployment is at the highest peak in our history. Of some five and one-half million Americans who are without jobs, more than one million have been searching for work for more than four months. And during each month some 150,000 workers are exhausting their already meager jobless benefit rights.

Nearly one-eighth of those who are without jobs live almost without hope in nearly one hundred especially depressed and troubled areas. The rest include new school graduates unable to use their talents, farmers forced to give up their part-time jobs which helped balance their family budgets, skilled and unskilled workers laid off in such important industries as metals, machinery, automobiles and apparel.

Our recovery from the 1958 recession, moreover, was anemic and incomplete. Our Gross National Product never regained its full potential. Unemployment never returned to normal levels. Maximum use of our national industrial capacity was never restored.

In short, the American economy is in trouble. The most resourceful industrialized country on earth ranks among the last in the rate of economic growth. Since last spring our economic growth rate has actually receded. Business investment is in a decline. Profits have fallen below predicted levels. Construction is off. A million unsold automobiles are in inventory. Fewer people are working – and the average work week has shrunk well below 40 hours. Yet prices have continued to rise – so that now too many Americans have less to spend for items that cost more to buy.

Economic prophecy is at best an uncertain art – as demonstrated by the prediction one year ago from this same podium that 1960 would be, and I quote, "the most prosperous year in our history." Nevertheless, forecasts of continued slack and only slightly reduced unemployment through 1961 and 1962 have been made with alarming unanimity – and this Administration does not intend to stand helplessly by.

We cannot afford to waste idle hours and empty plants while awaiting the end of the recession. We must show the world what a free economy can do – to reduce unemployment, to put unused capacity to work, to spur new productivity, and to foster higher economic growth within a range of sound fiscal policies and relative price stability.

I will propose to Congress within the next 14 days measures to improve unemployment compensation through temporary increases in duration on a self-supporting basis – to provide more food for the families of the unemployed, and to aid their needy children – to redevelop our areas of chronic labor surplus – to expand the services of the U.S. Employment Offices – to stimulate housing and construction – to secure more purchasing power for our lowest paid workers by raising and expanding the minimum wage – to offer tax incentives for sound plant investment – to increase the development of our natural resources – to encourage price stability – and to take other steps aimed at insuring a prompt recovery and paving the way for increased long-range growth. This is not a partisan program concentrating on our weaknesses – it is, I hope, a national program to realize our national strength.

II.

Efficient expansion at home, stimulating the new plant and technology that can make our goods more competitive, is also the key to the international balance of payments problem. Laying aside all alarmist talk and panicky solutions, let us put that knotty problem in its proper perspective.

It is true that, since 1958, the gap between the dollars we spend or invest abroad and the dollars returned to us has substantially widened. This overall deficit in our balance of payments increased by nearly $11 billion in the 3 years – and holders of dollars abroad converted them to gold in such a quantity as to cause a total outflow of nearly $5 billion of gold from our reserve. The 1959 deficit was caused in large part by the failure of our exports to penetrate foreign markets – the result both of restrictions on our goods and our own uncompetitive prices. The 1960 deficit, on the other hand, was more the result of an increase in private capital outflow seeking new opportunity, higher return or speculative advantage abroad.

Meanwhile this country has continued to bear more than its share of the West's military and foreign aid obligations. Under existing policies, another deficit of $2 billion is predicted for 1961 – and individuals in those countries whose dollar position once depended on these deficits for improvement now wonder aloud whether our gold reserves will remain sufficient to meet our own obligations.

All this is cause for concern – but it is not cause for panic. For our monetary and financial position remains exceedingly strong. Including our drawing rights in the International Monetary Fund and the gold reserve held as backing for our currency and Federal Reserve deposits, we have some $22 billion in total gold stocks and other international monetary reserves available – and I now pledge that their full strength stands behind the value of the dollar for use if needed.

Moreover, we hold large assets abroad – the total owed this nation far exceeds the claims upon our reserves – and our exports once again substantially exceed our imports.

In short, we need not—and we shall not — take any action to increase the dollar price of gold from $35 an ounce — to impose exchange controls — to reduce our anti-recession efforts — to fall back on restrictive trade policies — or to weaken our commitments around the world.

This Administration will not distort the value of the dollar in any fashion. And this is a commitment.

Prudence and good sense do require, however, that new steps be taken to ease the payments deficit and prevent any gold crisis. Our success in world affairs has long depended in part upon foreign confidence in our ability to pay. A series of executive orders, legislative remedies and cooperative efforts with our allies will get underway immediately — aimed at attracting foreign investment and travel to this country — promoting American exports, at stable prices and with more liberal government guarantees and financing — curbing tax and customs loopholes that encourage undue spending of private dollars abroad — and (through OECD, NATO and otherwise) sharing with our allies all efforts to provide for the common defense of the free world and the hopes for growth of the less developed lands. While the current deficit lasts, ways will be found to ease our dollar outlays abroad without placing the full burden on the families of men whom we have asked to serve our Flag overseas.

In short, whatever is required will be done to back up all our efforts abroad, and to make certain that, in the future as in the past, the dollar is as "sound as a dollar."

III.

But more than our exchange of international payments is out of balance. The current Federal budget for fiscal 1961 is almost certain to show a net deficit. The budget already submitted for fiscal 1962 will remain in balance only if the Congress enacts all the revenue measures requested — and only if an earlier and sharper up-turn in the economy than my economic advisers now think likely produces the tax revenues estimated. Nevertheless, a new Administration must of necessity build on the spending and revenue estimates already submitted. Within that framework, barring the development of urgent national defense needs or a worsening of the economy, it is my current intention to advocate a program of expenditures which, including revenues from a stimulation of the economy, will not of and by themselves unbalance the earlier Budget.

However, we will do what must be done. For our national household is cluttered with unfinished and neglected tasks. Our cities are being engulfed in squalor. Twelve long years after Congress declared our goal to be "a decent home and a suitable environment for every American family," we still have 25 million Americans living in substandard homes. A new housing program under a new Housing and Urban Affairs Department will be needed this year.

Our classrooms contain 2 million more children than they can properly have room for, taught by 90,000 teachers not properly qualified to teach. One third of our most promising high school graduates are financially unable to continue the development of their talents. The war babies of the 1940's, who overcrowded our schools in the 1950's, are now descending in 1960 upon our colleges — with two college students for every one, ten years from now — and our colleges are ill prepared. We lack the scientists, the engineers and the teachers our world obligations require. We have neglected oceanography, saline water conversion, and the basic research that lies at the root of all progress. Federal grants for both higher and public school education can no longer be delayed.

Medical research has achieved new wonders — but these wonders are too often beyond the reach of too many people, owing to a lack of income (particularly among the aged), a lack of hospital beds, a lack of nursing homes and a lack of doctors and dentists. Measures to provide health care for the aged under Social Security, and to increase the supply of both facilities and personnel, must be undertaken this year.

Our supply of clean water is dwindling. Organized and juvenile crimes cost the taxpayers millions of dollars each year, making it essential that we have improved enforcement and new legislative safeguards. The denial of constitutional rights to some of our fellow Americans on account of race — at the ballot box and elsewhere — disturbs the national conscience, and subjects us to the charge of world opinion that our democracy is not equal to the high promise of our heritage. Morality in private business has not been sufficiently spurred by morality in public business. A host of problems and projects in all 50 States, though not possible to include in this Message, deserves — and will receive — the attention of both the Congress and the Executive Branch. On most of these matters Messages will be sent to the Congress within the next two weeks.

IV.

But all these problems pale when placed beside those which confront us around the world. No man entering upon this office, regardless of his party, regardless of his previous service in Washington, could fail to be staggered upon learning — even in this brief 10 day period — the harsh enormity of the trials through which we must pass in the next four years. Each day the crises multiply. Each day their solution grows more difficult. Each day we draw nearer the hour of maximum danger, as weapons spread and hostile forces grow stronger. I feel I must inform the Congress that our analyses over the last ten days make it clear that — in each of the principal areas of crisis — the tide of events has been running out and time has not been our friend.

In Asia, the relentless pressures of the Chinese Communists menace the security of the entire area — from the borders of India and South Viet Nam to the jungles of Laos, struggling to protect its newly-won independence. We seek in Laos what we seek in all Asia, and, indeed, in all of the world — freedom for the people and independence for the government. And this nation shall persevere in our pursuit of these objectives.

In Africa, the Congo has been brutally torn by civil strife, political unrest and public disorder. We shall continue to support the heroic efforts of the United Nations to restore peace and order — efforts which are now endangered by mounting tensions, unsolved problems, and decreasing support from many member states.

In Latin America, Communist agents seeking to exploit that region's peaceful revolution of hope have established a base on Cuba, only 90 miles from our shores. Our objection with Cuba is not over the people's drive for a better life. Our objection is to their domination by foreign and domestic tyrannies. Cuban social and economic reform should be encouraged. Questions of economic and trade policy can always be negotiated. But Communist domination in this Hemisphere can never be negotiated.

We are pledged to work with our sister republics to free the Americas of all such foreign domination and all tyranny, working toward the goal of a free hemisphere of free governments, extending from Cape Horn to the Arctic Circle.

In Europe our alliances are unfulfilled and in some disarray. The unity of NATO has been weakened by economic rivalry and partially eroded by national interest. It has not yet fully mobilized its resources nor fully achieved a common outlook. Yet no Atlantic power can meet on its own the mutual problems now facing us in defense, foreign aid, monetary reserves, and a host of other areas; and our close ties with those whose hopes and interest we share are among this Nation's most powerful assets.

Our greatest challenge is still the world that lies beyond the Cold War — but the first great obstacle is still our relations with the Soviet Union and Communist China. We must never be lulled into believing that either power has yielded its ambitions for world domination — ambitions which they forcefully restated only a short time ago. On the contrary, our task is to convince them that aggression and subversion will not be profitable routes to pursue these ends. Open and peaceful competition — for prestige, for markets, for scientific achievement, even for men's minds — is something else again. For if Freedom and Communism were to compete for man's allegiance in a world at peace, I would look to the future with ever increasing confidence.

To meet this array of challenges — to fulfill the role we cannot avoid on the world scene — we must reexamine and revise our whole arsenal of tools: military, economic and political.

One must not overshadow the other. On the Presidential Coat of Arms, the American eagle holds in his right talon the olive branch, while in his left he holds a bundle of arrows. We intend to give equal attention to both.

First, we must strengthen our military tools. We are moving into a period of uncertain risk and great commitment in which both the military and diplomatic possibilities require a Free World force so powerful as to make any aggression clearly futile. Yet in the past, lack of consistent, coherent military strategy, the absence of basic assumptions about our national requirements and the faulty estimates and duplication arising from inter-service rivalries have all made it difficult to assess accurately how adequate — or inadequate — our defenses really are.

I have, therefore, instructed the Secretary of Defense to reappraise our entire defense strategy — our ability to fulfill our commitments — the effectiveness, vulnerability, and dispersal of our strategic bases, forces and warning systems — the efficiency and economy of our operation and organization — the elimination of obsolete bases and installations — and the adequacy, modernization and mobility of our present conventional and nuclear forces and weapons systems in the light of present and future dangers. I have asked for preliminary conclusions by the end of February — and I then shall recommend whatever legislative, budgetary or executive action is needed in the light of these conclusions.

In the meantime, I have asked the Defense Secretary to initiate immediately three new steps most clearly needed now:

First, I have directed prompt attention to increase our air-lift capacity. Obtaining additional air transport mobility — and obtaining it now — will better assure the ability of our conventional forces to respond, with discrimination and speed, to any problem at any spot on the globe at any moment's notice. In particular it will enable us to meet any deliberate effort to avoid or divert our forces by starting limited wars in widely scattered parts of the globe. . . .

Secondly, we must improve our economic tools. Our role is essential and unavoidable in the construction of a sound and expanding economy for the entire non-communist world, helping other nations build the strength to meet their own problems, to satisfy their own aspirations — to surmount their own dangers. The problems in achieving this goal are towering and unprecedented — the response must be towering and unprecedented as well, much as Lend-Lease and the Marshall Plan were in earlier years, which brought such fruitful results. . . .

Third, we must sharpen our political and diplomatic tools — the means of cooperation and agreement on which an enforceable world order must ultimately rest.

I have already taken steps to coordinate and expand our disarmament effort — to increase our programs of research and study — and to make arms control a central goal of our national policy under my direction. The deadly arms race and the huge resources it absorbs have too long overshadowed all else we must do. We must prevent that arms race from spreading to new nations, to new nuclear powers and to the reaches of outer space. We must make certain that our negotiators are better informed and better prepared — to formulate workable proposals of our own and to make sound judgments about the proposals of others . . . .

Finally, this Administration intends to explore promptly all possible areas of cooperation with the Soviet Union and other nations "to invoke the wonders of science instead of its terrors." Specifically, I now invite all nations — including the Soviet Union — to join with us in developing a weather prediction program, in a new communications satellite program and in preparation for probling the distant planets of Mars and Venus, probes which may someday unlock the deepest secrets of the universe.

Today this country is ahead in the science and technology of space, while the Soviet Union is ahead in the capacity to lift large vehicles into orbit. Both nations would help themselves as well as other nations by removing these endeavors from the bitter and wasteful competition of the Cold War. The United States would be willing to join with the Soviet Union and the scientists of all nations in a greater effort to make the fruits of this new knowledge available to all — and, beyond that, in an effort to extend farm technology to hungry nations — to wipe out disease — to increase the exchanges of scientists and their knowledge — and to make our own laboratories available to technicians of other lands who lack the facilities to pursue their own work. Where nature makes natural allies of us all, we can demonstrate that beneficial relations are possible even with those with whom we most deeply disagree — and this must someday be the basis of world peace and world law.

V.

I have commented on the state of the domestic economy, our balance of payments, our Federal and social budget and the state of the world. I would like to conclude with a few remarks about the state of the Executive branch. We have found it full of honest and useful public servants — but their capacity to act decisively at the exact time action is needed has too often been muffled in the morass of committees, timidities and fictitious theroies which have created a growing gap between decision and execution, between planning and reality. In a time of rapidly deteriorating situations at home and abroad, this is bad for the public service and particularly bad for the country; and we mean to make a change.

I have pledged myself and my colleagues in the cabinet to a continuous encouragement of initiative, responsibility and energy in serving the public interest. Let every public servant know, whether his post is high or low, that a man's rank and reputation in this Administration will be determined by the size of the job he does, and not by the size of his staff, his office or his budget. Let it be clear that this Administration recognizes the value of dissent and daring — that we greet healthy change. Let the public service be a proud and lively career. And let every man and woman who works in any area of our national government, in any branch, at any level, be able to say with pride and with honor in future years: "I served the United States government in that hour of our nation's need."

For only with complete dedication by us all to the national interest can we bring our country through the troubled years that lie ahead. Our problems are critical. The tide is unfavorable. The news will be worse before it is better. And while hoping and working for the best, we should prepare ourselves now for the worst.

We cannot escape our dangers — neither must we let them drive us into panic or narrow isolation. In many areas of the world where the balance of power already rests with our adversaries, the forces of freedom are sharply divided. It is one of the ironies of our time that the techniques of a harsh and repressive system should be able to instill discipline and ardor in its servants — while the blessings of liberty have too often stood for privilege, materialism and a life of ease.

But I have a different view of liberty.

Life in 1961 will not be easy. Wishing it, predicting it, even asking for it, will not make it so. There will be further setbacks before the tide is turned. But turn it we must. The hopes of all mankind rest upon us — not simply upon those of us in this chamber, but upon the peasant in Laos, the fisherman in Nigeria, the exile from Cuba, the spirit that moves every man and Nation who shares our hopes for freedom and the future. And in the final analysis, they rest most of all upon the pride and perseverance of our fellow citizens of the great Republic.

In the words of a great President, whose birthday we honor today, closing his final State of the Union Message sixteen years ago, "We pray that we may be worthy of the unlimited opportunities that God had given us."

CUBA AND THE BAY OF PIGS INVASION
April 20, 1961

Speaking to the American Society of Newspaper Editors
only a day after Castro had crushed a band of United
States-supported Cuban exiles attempting to overthrow
the Cuban government, Kennedy was obviously disturbed
and sobered by this early failure in his foreign policy.
His resolve to avoid future such defeats — in Cuba or
in South Vietnam — was made clear.

The President of a great democracy such as ours, and the editors of great newspapers such as yours, owe a common obligation to the people: an obligation to present the facts, to present them with candor, and to present them in perspective. It is with that obligation in mind that I have decided in the last 24 hours to discuss briefly at this time the recent events in Cuba.

On that unhappy island, as in so many other arenas of the contest for freedom, the news has grown worse instead of better. I have emphasized before that this was a struggle of Cuban patriots against a Cuban dictator. While we could not be expected to hide our sympathies, we made it repeatedly clear that the armed forces of this country would not intervene in any way.

Any unilateral American intervention, in the absence of an external attack upon ourselves or an ally, would have been contrary to our traditions and to our international obligations. But let the record show that our restraint is not inexhaustible. Should it ever appear that the inter-American doctrine of non-interference merely conceals or excuses a policy of nonaction — if the nations of this Hemisphere should fail to meet their commitments against outside Communist penetration — then I want it clearly understood that this Government will not hesitate in meeting its primary obligations which are to the security of our Nation!

Should that time ever come, we do not intend to be lectured on "intervention" by those whose character was stamped for all time on the bloody streets of Budapest! Nor would we expect or accept the same outcome which this small band of gallant Cuban refugees must have known that they were chancing, determined as they were against heavy odds to pursue their courageous attempts to regain their Island's freedom.

But Cuba is not an island unto itself; and our concern is not ended by mere expressions of nonintervention or regret. This is not the first time in either ancient or recent history that a small band of freedom fighters has engaged the armor of totalitarianism.

It is not the first time that Communist tanks have rolled over gallant men and women fighting to redeem the independence of their homeland. Nor is it by any means the final episode in the eternal struggle of liberty against tyranny, anywhere on the face of the globe, including Cuba itself.

Mr. Castro has said that these were mercenaries. According to press reports, the final message to be relayed from the refugee forces on the beach came from the rebel commander when asked if he wished to be evacuated. His answer was: "I will never leave this country." That is not the reply of a mercenary. He has gone now to join in the mountains countless other guerrilla fighters, who are equally determined that the dedication of those who gave their lives shall not be forgotten, and that Cuba must not be abandoned to the Communists. And we do not intend to abandon it either!

The Cuban people have not yet spoken their final piece. And I have no doubt that they and their Revolutionary Council, led by Dr. Cardona — and members of the families of the Revolutionary council, I am informed by the Doctor yesterday, are involved themselves in the Islands — will continue to speak up for a free and independent Cuba.

Meanwhile we will not accept Mr. Castro's attempts to blame this nation for the hatred which his onetime supporters now regard his repression. But there are from this sobering episode useful lessons for us all to learn. Some may be still obscure, and await further information. Some are clear today.

First, it is clear that the forces of communism are not to be underestimated, in Cuba or anywhere else in the world. The advantages of a police state — its use of mass terror and arrests to prevent the spread of free dissent — cannot be overlooked by those who expect the fall of every fanatic tyrant. If the self-discipline of the free cannot match the iron discipline of the mailed first — in economic, political, scientific and all the other kinds of struggles as well as the military — then the peril to freedom will continue to rise.

Secondly, it is clear that this Nation, in concert with all the free nations of this hemisphere, must take an ever closer and more realistic look at the menace of external Communist intervention and domination in Cuba. The American people are not complacent about Iron Curtain tanks and planes less than 90 miles from their shore. But a nation of Cuba's size is less a threat to our survival than it is a base for subverting the survival of other free nations throughout the hemisphere. It is not primarily our interest or our security but theirs which is now, today, in the greater peril. It is for their sake as well as our own that we must show our will.

The evidence is clear — and the hour is late. We and our Latin friends will have to face the fact that we cannot postpone any longer the real issue of survival of freedom in this hemisphere itself. On that issue, unlike perhpas some others, there can be no middle ground. Together we must build a hemisphere where freedom can flourish; and where any free nation under outside attack of any kind can be assured that all of our resources stand ready to respond to any request for assistance.

Third, and finally, it is clearer than ever that we face a relentless struggle in every corner of the globe that goes far beyond the clash of armies or even nuclear armaments. The armies are there, and in large number. The nuclear armaments are there. But they serve primarily as the shield behind which subversion, infiltration, and a host of other tactics steadily advance, picking off vulnerable areas one by one in situations which do not permit our own armed intervention.

Power is the hallmark of this offensive — power and discipline and deceit. The legitimate discontent of yearning people is exploited. The legitimate trappings of self-determination are employed. But once in power, all talk of discontent is repressed, all self-determination disappears, and the promise of a revolution of hope is betrayed, as in Cuba, into a reign of terror. Those who on instruction staged automatic "riots" in the streets of free nations over the efforts of a small group of young Cubans to regain their freedom should recall the long roll call of refugees who cannot now go back — to Hungary, to North Korea, to North Viet-Nam, to East Germany, or to Poland, or to any of the other lands from which a steady stream of refugees pours forth, in eloquent testimony to the cruel oppression now holding sway in their homeland.

We dare not fail to see the insidious nature of this new and deeper struggle. We dare not fail to grasp the new concepts, the new tools, the new sense of urgency we will need to combat it — whether in Cuba or South Viet-Nam. And we dare not fail to relize that this struggle is taking place every day, without fanfare, in thousands of villages and markets — day and night — and in classrooms all over the globe.

The message of Cuba, of Laos, of the rising din of Communist voices in Asia and Latin America — these messages are all the same. The complacent, the self-indulgent, the soft societies are about to be swept away with the debris of history. Only the strong, only the industrious, only the determined, only the courageous, only the visionary who determine the real nature of our struggle can possibly survive.

No greater task faces this country or this administration. No other challenge is more deserving of our every effort and energy. Too long we hve fixed our eyes on traditional military needs, on armies prepared to cross borders, on missiles poised for flight. Now it should be clear that this is no longer enough — that our security may be lost piece by piece, country by country, without the firing of a single missile or the crossing of a single border.

We intend to profit from this lesson. We intend to reexamine and reorient our forces of all kinds — our tactics and our institutions here in this community. We intend to intensify our efforts for a struggle in many ways more difficult than war, where disappointment will often accompany us.

For I am convinced that we in this country and in the free world possess the necessary resource, and the skill, and the added strength that comes from a belief in the freedom of man. And I am equally convinced that history will record the fact that this bitter struggle reached its climax in the late 1950's and the early 1960's. Let me then make clear as the President of the United States that I am determined upon our system's survival and success, regardless of the cost and regardless of the peril!

LETTER TO NGO DINH DIEM
December 15, 1961

*Diem, the strong-willed President of South Vietnam, had
asked the United States for further assistance against
"the forces of International Communism." Kennedy re-
sponded favorably, not only expressing agreement with
Diem that Hanoi was guilty of "outside" aggression,
but also pledging additional assistance to the South
Vietnamese government.*

I have received your recent letter in which you described so co-
gently the dangerous condition caused by North Viet-Nam's efforts to
take over your country. The situation in your embattled country is
well known to me and to the American people. We have been deeply
disturbed by the assault on your country. Our indignation has mounted
as the deliberate savagery of the Communist program of assassination, kidnapping and wanton violence became clear.

Your letter underlines what our own information has convincingly
shown — that the campaign of force and terror now being waged a-
gainst your people and your Government is supported and directed
from the outside by the authorities at Hanoi. They have thus violated
the provisions of the Geneva Accords designed to ensure peace in
Viet-Nam and to which they bound themselves in 1954.

At that time, the United States, although not a party to the Accords,
declared that it "would view any renewal of the aggression in violation of the agreements with grave concern and as seriously threaten-
ing international peace and security." We continue to maintain that
view.

In accordance with that declaration, and in response to your request,
we are prepared to help the Republic of Viet-Nam to protect its people
and to preserve its independence. We shall promptly increase our
assistance to your defense effort as well as help relieve the destruction of the floods which you describe. I have already given the orders
to get these programs underway.

The United States, like the Republic of Viet-Nam, remains devoted
to the cause of peace and our primary purpose is to help your people
maintain their independence. If the Communist authorities in North
Viet-Nam will stop their campaign to destroy the Republic of Viet-
Nam, the measures we are taking to assist your defense efforts will
no longer be necessary. We shall seek to persuade the Communists to
give up their attempts of force and subversion. In any case, we are
confident that the Vietnamese people will preserve their independence
and gain the peace and prosperity for which they have sought so hard
and so long.

SECOND ANNUAL MESSAGE TO CONGRESS
January 11, 1962

After a year in office, Kennedy's primary concern was still foreign affairs. But he emphasized in this message that diplomatic problems could not be solved without domestic reforms. Specifically, he pointed to the need for more liberal trade and tariff policies; legislation broadening civil rights; price and wage stability; and a strengthened educational system.

Members of the Congress, the Constitution makes us not rivals for power but partners for progress. We are all trustees for the American people, custodians of the American heritage. It is my task to report the State of the Union — to improve it is the task of us all.

In the past year, I have travelled not only across our own land but to other lands — to the North and the South, and across the seas. And I have found — as I am sure you have, in your travels — that people everywhere, in spite of occasional disappointments, look to us — not to our wealth or power, but to the splendor of our ideals. For our Nation is commissioned by history to be either an observer of freedom's failure or the cause of its success. Our overriding obligation in the months ahead is to fulfill the world's hopes by fulfilling our own faith.

I. STRENGTHENING THE ECONOMY

That task must begin at home. For if we cannot fulfill our own ideals here, we cannot expect others to accept them. And when the youngest child alive today has grown to the cares of manhood, our position in the world will be determined first of all by what provisions we make today — for his education, his health, and his opportunities for a good home and a good job and a good life.

At home, we began the year in the valley of recession — we completed it on the high road of recovery and growth. With the help of new congressionally approved or administratively increased stimulants to our economy, the number of major surplus labor areas has declined from 101 to 60; nonagricultural employment has increased by more than a million jobs; and the average factory work-week has risen to well over 40 hours. At year's end the economy which Mr. Khrushchev once called a "stumbling horse" was racing to new records in consumer spending, labor income, and industrial production.

We are gratified — but we are not satisfied. Too many unemployed are still looking for the blessings of prosperity. As those who leave our schools and farms demand new jobs, automation takes old jobs away. To expand our growth and job opportunities, I urge on the Congress three measures:

(1) First, the Manpower Training and Development Act, to stop the waste of able bodied men and women who want to work, but whose only skill has been replaced by a machine, or moved with a mill, or shut down with a mine;

(2) Second, the Youth Employment Opportunities Act, to help train and place not only the one million young Americans who are both out of school and out of work, but the twenty-six million young Americans entering the labor market in this decade; and

(3) Third, the 8 percent tax credit for investment in machinery and equipment, which, combined with planned revisions of depreciation allowances, will spur our modernization, our growth, and our ability to compete abroad.

Moreover — pleasant as it may be to bask in the warmth of recovery — let us not forget that we have suffered three recessions in the last 7 years. The time to repair the roof is when the sun is shining — by filling three basic gaps in our anti-recession protection. We need:

(1) First, Presidential standby authority, subject to congressional veto, to adjust personal income tax rates downward within a specified range and time, to slow down an economic decline before it has dragged us all down;

(2) Second, Presidential standby authority, upon a given rise in the rate of unemployments, to accelerate Federal and federally-aided capital improvement programs; and

(3) Third, a permanent strengthening of our unemployment compensation system — to maintain for our fellow citizens searching for a job who cannot find it, their purchasing power and their living standards without constant resort — as we have seen in recent years by the Congress and the administrations — to temporary supplements.

If we enact this six-part program, we can show the whole world that a free economy need not be an unstable economy — that a free system need not leave men unemployed — and that a free society is not only the most productive but the most stable form of organization yet fashioned by man.

II. FIGHTING INFLATION

But recession is only one enemy of a free economy — inflation is another. Last year, 1961, despite rising production and demand, consumer prices held almost steady — and wholesale prices declined. This is the best record of overall price stability of any comparable period of recovery since the end of World War II.

Inflation too often follows in the shadow of growth — while price stability is made easy by stagnation or controls. But we mean to maintain both stability and growth in a climate of freedom.

Our first line of defense against inflation is the good sense and public spirit of business and labor — keeping their total increases in wages and profits in step with productivity. There is no single statistical test to guide each company and each union. But I strongly urge them — for their country's interest, and for their own — to apply the test of the public interest to these transactions.

Within this same framework of growth and wage-price stability:

— This administration has helped keep our economy competitive by widening the access of small business to credit and Government contracts, and by stepping up the drive against monopoly, price-fixing, and racketeering;

— We will submit a Federal Pay Reform bill aimed at giving our classified, postal, and other employees new pay scales more comparable to those of private industry;

— We are holding the fiscal 1962 budget deficit far below the level incurred after the last recession in 1958; and, finally,

— I am submitting for fiscal 1963 a balanced Federal Budget.

This is a joint responsibility, requiring Congressional cooperation on appropriations, and on three sources of income in particular:

(1) First, an increase in postal rates, to end the postal deficit;

(2) Secondly, passage of the tax reforms previously urged, to remove unwarranted tax preferences, and to apply to dividends and to interest the same withholding requirements we have long applied to wages; and

(3) Third, extension of the present excise and corporation tax rates, except for those changes — which will be recommended in a message — affecting transportation.

III. GETTING AMERICA MOVING

But a stronger nation and economy require more than a balanced Budget. They require progress in those programs that spur our growth and fortify our strength.

CITIES

A strong America depends on its cities — America's glory, and sometimes America's shame. To substitute sunlight for congestion and progress for decay, we have stepped up existing urban renewal and housing programs, and launched new ones — redoubled the attack on water pollution — speeded aid to airports, hospitals, highways, and our declining mass transit systems — and secured new weapons to combat organized crime, racketeering, and youth delinquency, assisted by the coordinated and hard-hitting efforts of our investigative services: the FBI, the Internal Revenue, the Bureau of Narcotics, and many others. We shall need further anti-crime, mass transit, and transportation legislation — and new tools to fight air pollution. And with all this effort under way, both equity and commonsense require that our nation's urban areas — containing three-fourths of our population — sit as equals at the Cabinet table. I urge a new Department of Urban Affairs and Housing.

AGRICULTURE AND RESOURCES

A strong America also depends on its farms and natural resources. American farmers took heart in 1961 — from a billion dollar rise in farm income — and from a hopeful start on reducing the farm surpluses. But we are still operating under a patchwork accumulation of old laws, which cost us $1 billion a year in CCC carrying charges alone, yet fail to halt rural poverty or boost farm earnings.

Our task is to master and turn to fully fruitful ends the magnificent productivity of our farms and farmers. The revolution on our own countryside stands in the sharpest contrast to the repeated farm failures of the Communist nations and is a source of pride to us all. Since 1950 our agricultural output per man-hour has actually doubled! Without new, realistic measures, it will someday swamp our farmers and our taxpayers in a national scandal or a farm depression.

I will, therefore, submit to the Congress a new comprehensive farm program — tailored to fit the use of our land and the supplies of each crop to the long-range needs of the sixties — and designed to prevent chaos in the sixties with a program of commonsense.

We also need for the sixties — if we are to bequeath our full national estate to our heirs — a new long-range conservation and recreation program — expansion of our superb national parks and forests — preservation of our authentic wilderness areas — new starts on water and power projects as our population steadily increases — and expanded REA generation and transmission loans.

CIVIL RIGHTS

But America stands for progress in human rights as well as economic affairs, and a strong America requires the assurance of full and equal rights to all its citizens, of any race or of any color. This administration has shown as never before how much could be done through the full use of Executive powers – through the enforcement of laws already passed by the Congress – through persuasion, negotiation, and litigation, to secure the constitutional rights of all: the right to vote, the right to travel without hindrance across State lines, and the right to free public education.

I issued last March a comprehensive order to guarantee the right to equal employment opportunity in all Federal agencies and contractors. The Vice President's Committee thus created has done much, including the voluntary "Plans for Progress' which, in all sections of the country, are achieving a quiet but striking success in opening up to all races new professional, supervisory, and other job opportunities.

But there is much more to be done – by the Executive, by the courts, and by the Congress. Among the bills now pending before you, on which the executive departments will comment in detail, are appropriate methods of strengthening these basic rights which have our full support. The right to vote, for example, should no longer be denied through such arbitrary devices on a local level, sometimes abused, such as literacy tests and poll taxes. As we approach the 100th anniversary, next January, of the Emancipation Proclamation, let the acts of every branch of the Government – and every citizen – portray that "righteousness does exalt a nation."

HEALTH AND WELFARE

Finally, a strong America cannot neglect the aspirations of its citizens – the welfare of the needy, the health care of the elderly, the education of the young. For we are not developing the Nation's wealth for its own sake. Wealth is the means – and people are the ends. All our material riches will avail us little if we do not use them to expand the opportunities of our people.

Last year, we improved the diet of needy people – provided more hot lunches and fresh milk to school children – built more college dormitories – and, for the elderly, expanded private housing, nursing homes, health services, and social security. But we have just begun.

To help those least fortunate of all, I am recommending a new public welfare program, stressing services instead of support, rehabilitation instead of relief, and training for useful work instead of prolonged dependency.

To relieve the critical shortage of doctors and dentists – and this is a matter which should concern us all – and expand research, I urge action to aid medical and dental colleges and scholarships and to establish new National Institutes of Health.

To take advantage of modern vaccination achievements, I am proposing a mass immunization program, aimed at the virtual elimination of such ancient enemies of our children as polio, diptheria, whooping cough, and tetanus.

To protect our consumers from the careless and the unscrupulous, I shall recommend improvements in the Food and Drug laws — strengthening inspection and standards, halting unsafe and worthless products, preventing misleading labels, and cracking down on the illicit sale of habit-forming drugs.

But in matters of health, no piece of unfinished business is more important or more urgent than the enactment under the social security system of health insurace for the aged.

For our older citizens have longer and more frequent illnesses, higher hospital and medical bills and too little income to pay them. Private health insurance helps very few — for its cost is high and its coverage limited. Public welfare cannot help those too proud to seek relief but hard-pressed to pay their own bills. Nor can their children or grandchildren always sacrifice their own health budgets to meet this constant drain.

Social security has long helped to meet the hardships of retirement, death, and disability. I now urge that its coverage be extended without further delay to provide health insurance for the elderly.

EDUCATION

Equally important to our strength is the quality of our education. Eight million adult Americans are classified as functionally illiterate. This is a disturbing figure — reflected in Selective Service rejection rates — reflected in welfare rolls and crime rates. And I shall recommend bills to improve educational quality, to stimulate the arts, and, at the college level, to provide Federal loans for the construction of academic facilities and federally financed scholarships.

If this Nation is to grow in wisdom and strength, then every able high school graduate should have the opportunity to develop his talents. Yet nearly half lack either the funds or the facilities to attend college. Enrollments are going to double in our colleges in the short space of 10 years. The annual cost per student is skyrocketing to astronomical levels — now averaging $1,650 a year, although almost half of our families earn less than $5,000. They cannot afford such costs — but this Nation cannot afford to maintain its military power and neglect its brainpower.

But excellence in education must begin at the elementary level. I sent to the Congress last year a proposal for Federal aid to public school construction and teachers' salaries. I believe that bill, which passed the Senate and received House Committee approval, offered the minimum amount required by our needs and — in terms of across-the-board aid — the maximum scope permitted by our Constitution. I therefore see no reason to weaken or withdraw that bill: and I urge its passage at this session.

"Civilization," said H.G. Wells, "is a race between education and catastrophe." It is up to you in this Congress to determine the winner of that race. . . .

IV. OUR GOALS ABROAD

All of these efforts at home give meaning to our efforts abroad. Since the close of the Second World War, a global civil war has divided and tormented mankind. But it is not our military might, or our higher standard of living, that has most distinguished us from our adversaries. It is our belief that the state is the servant of the citizen and not his master.

This basic clash of ideas and wills is but one of the forces re-shaping our globe — swept as it is by the tides of hope and fear, by crises in the headlines today that become mere footnotes tomorrow. Both the successes and the setbacks of the past year remain on our agenda of unfinished business. For every apparent blessing contains the seeds of danger — every area of trouble gives out a ray of hope — and the one unchangeable certainty is that nothing is certain or unchangeable.

Yet our basic goal remains the same: a peaceful world community of free and independent states — free to choose their own future and their own system, so long as it does not threaten the freedom of others.

Some may choose forms and ways that we would not choose for ourselves — but it is not for us that they are choosing. We can welcome diversity — the Communists cannot. For we offer a world of choice — they offer the world of coercion. And the way of the past shows clearly that freedom, not coercion, is the wave of the future. At times our goal has been obscured by crisis or endangered by conflict — but it draws sustenance from five basic sources of strength:

— the moral and physical strength of the United States;

— the united strength of the Atlantic Community;

— the regional strength of our Hemispheric relations;

— the creative strength of our efforts in the new and developing nations; and

— the peace-keeping strength of the United Nations.

V. OUR MILITARY STRENGTH

Our moral and physical strength begins at home as already discussed. But it includes our military strength as well. So long as fanaticism and fear brood over the affairs of men, we must arm to deter others from aggression.

In the past 12 months our military posture has steadily improved. We increased the previous defense budget by 15 percent — not in the expectation of war but for the preservation of peace. We more than doubled our acquisition rate of Polaris submarines — we doubled the production capacity for Minuteman missiles — and increased by 50 percent the number of manned bombers standing ready on a 15 minute alert. This year the combined force levels planned under our new Defense budget — including nearly three hundred additional Polaris and Minuteman missiles — have been precisely calculated to insure the continuing strength of our nuclear deterrent.

But our strength may be tested at many levels. We intend to have at all times the capacity to resist non-nuclear or limited attacks — as a complement to our nuclear capacity, not as a substitute. We have rejected any all-or-nothing posture which would leave no choice but inglorious retreat or unlimited retaliation.

Thus we have doubled the number of ready combat divisions in the Army's strategic reserve — increased our troops in Europe — built up the Marines — added new sealift and airlift capacity — modernized our weapons and ammunition — expanded our anti-guerrilla forces — and increased the active fleet by more than 70 vessels and our tactical air forces by nearly a dozen wings.

Because we needed to reach this higher long-term level of readiness more quickly, 155,000 members of the Reserve and National Guard were activated under the Act of this Congress. Some disruptions and distress were inevitable. But the overwhelming majority bear their burdens — and their Nation's burdens — with admirable and traditional devotion.

In the coming year, our reserve programs will be revised — two Army Divisions will, I hope, replace those Guard Divisions on duty — and substantial other increases will boost our Air Force fighter units, the procurement of equipment, and our continental defense and warning efforts. The Nation's first serious civil defense shelter program is under way, identifying, marking, and stocking 50 million spaces; and I urge your approval of Federal incentives for the construction of public fall-out shelters in schools and hospitals and similar centers.

VI. THE UNITED NATIONS

But arms alone are not enough to keep the peace — it must be kept by men. Our instrument and our hope is the United Nations — and I see little merit in the impatience of those who would abandon this imperfect world instrument because they dislike our imperfect world. For the troubles of a world organization merely reflect the troubles of the world itself. And if the organization is weakened, these troubles can only increase. We may not always agree with every detailed action taken by every voting majority. But as an institution, it should have in the future, as it has had in the past since its inception, no stronger or more faithful member than the United States of America.

In 1961 the peace-keeping strength of the United Nations was reinforced. And those who preferred or predicted its demise, envisioning a troika in the seat of Hammarskjold — or Red China inside the Assembly — have seen instead a new vigor, under a new Secretary General and a fully independent Secretariat. In making plans for a new forum and principles on disarmament — for peace-keeping in outer space — for a decade of development effort — the UN fulfilled its Charter's lofty aim. . . .

With the approval of this Congress, we have undertaken in the past year a great new effort in outer space. Our aim is not simply to be first on the moon, any more than Charles Lindbergh's real aim was to be the first to Paris. His aim was to develop the techniques of our own country and other countries in the field of air and the atmosphere, and our objective in making this effort, which we hope will place one of our citizens on the moon, is to develop in a new frontier of science, commerce and cooperation, the position of the United States and the Free World.

This Nation belongs among the first to explore it, and among the first — if not the first — we shall be. We are offering our know-how and our cooperation to the United Nations. Our satellites will soon be providing other nations with improved weather observations. And I shall soon send to the Congress a measure to govern the financing and operation of an International Communications Satellite system, in a manner consistent with the public interest and our foreign policy.

But peace in space will help us naught once peace on earth is gone. World order will be secured only when the whole world has laid down these weapons which seem to offer us present security but threaten the future survival of the human race. That armistice day seems very far away. The vast resources of this planet are being devoted more and more to the means of destroying, instead of enriching, human life.

But the world was not meant to be a prison in which man awaits his execution. Nor has mankind survived the tests and trials of thousands of years to surrender everything — including its existence — now. This Nation has the will and the faith to make a supreme effort to break the log jam on disarmament and nuclear tests — and we will persist until we prevail, until the rule of law has replaced the ever dangerous use of force.

VII. LATIN AMERICA

I turn now to a prospect of great promise: our Hemispheric relations. The Alliance for Progress is being rapidly transformed from proposal to program. Last month in Latin America I saw for myself the quickening of hope, the revival of confidence, the new trust in our country — among workers and farmers as well as diplomats. We have pledged our help in speeding their economic, educational, and social progress. The Latin American Republics have in turn pledged a new and strenuous effort of self-help and self-reform.

To support this historic undertaking, I am proposing — under the authority contained in the bills of the last session of the Congress — a special long-term Alliance for Progress fund of $3 billion. Combined with our Food for Peace, Export-Import Bank, and other resources, this will provide more than $1 billion a year in new support for the Alliance. In addition, we have increased twelvefold our Spanish and Portuguese-language broadcasting in Latin America, and improved Hemispheric trade and defense. And while the blight of communism has been increasingly exposed and isolated in the Americas, liberty has scored a gain. The people of the Dominican Republic, with our firm encouragement and help, and those of our sister Republics of this Hemisphere are safely passing through the treacherous course from dictatorship through disorder towards democracy.

VIII. THE NEW AND DEVELOPING NATIONS

Our efforts to help other new or developing nations, and to strengthen their stand for freedom, have also made progress. A newly unified Agency for International Development is reorienting our foreign assistance to emphasize long-term development loans instead of grants, more economic aid instead of military, individual plans to meet the individual needs of the nations, and new standards on what they must do to marshal their own resources.

A newly conceived Peace Corps is winning friends and helping people in fourteen countries — supplying trained and dedicated young men and women, to give these new nations a hand in building a society, and a glimpse of the best that is in our country. If there is a problem here, it is that we cannot supply the spontaneous and mounting demand.

A newly-expanded Food for Peace Program is feeding the hungry of many lands with the abundance of our productive farms — providing lunches for children in school, wages for economic development, relief for the victims of flood and famine, and a better diet for millions whose daily bread is their chief concern.

These programs help people; and, by helping people, they help freedom. The views of their governments may sometimes be very different from ours — but events in Africa, the Middle East, and Eastern

Europe teach us never to write off any nation as lost to the Communists. That is the lesson of our time. We support the independence of those newer or weaker states whose history, geography, economy or lack of power impels them to remain outside "entangling Alliances" — as we did for more than a century. For the independence of nations is a bar to the Communists' "grand design" — it is the basis of our own.

In the past year, for example, we have urged a neutral and independent Laos — regained there a common policy with our major allies — and insisted that a cease-fire precede negotiations. While a workable formula for supervising its independence is still to be achieved, both the spread of war — which might have involved this country also — and a Communist occupation have thus far been prevented.

A satisfactory settlement in Laos would also help to achieve and safeguard the peace in Viet-Nam — where the foe is increasing his tactics of terror — where our own efforts have been stepped up — and where the local government has initiated new programs and reforms to broaden the base of resistance. The systematic aggression now bleeding that country is not a "war of liberation" — for Viet-Nam is already free. It is a war of attempted subjugation — and it will be resisted.

IX. THE ATLANTIC COMMUNITY

Finally, the united strength of the Atlantic Community has flourished in the last year under severe tests. NATO has increased both the number and the readiness of its air, ground, and naval units — both its nuclear and non-nuclear capabilities. Even greater efforts by all its members are still required. Nevertheless our unity of purpose and will has been, I believe, immeasurably strengthened.

The threat to the brave city of Berlin remains. In these last 6 months the Allies have made it unmistakably clear that our presence in Berlin, our free access thereto, and the freedom of two million West Berliners would not be surrendered either to force or through appeasement — and to maintain those rights and obligations, we are prepared to talk, when appropriate, and to fight, if necessary. Every member of NATO stands with us in a common commitment to preserve this symbol of free man's will to remain free.

I cannot now predict the course of future negotiations over Berlin. I can only say that we are sparing no honorable effort to find a peaceful and mutually acceptable resolution of this problem. I believe such a resolution can be found, and with it an improvement in our relations with the Soviet Union, if only the leaders in the Kremlin will recognize the basic rights and interests involved, and the interest of all mankind in peace.

But the Atlantic Community is no longer concerned with purely military aims. As its common undertakings grow at an ever-increasing pace, we are, and increasingly will be, partners in aid, trade, defense, diplomacy, and monetary affairs.

The emergence of the new Europe is being matched by the emergence of new ties across the Atlantic. It is a matter of undramtic daily cooperation in hundreds of workaday tasks: of currencies kept in effective relation, of development loans meshed together, of standardized weapons, and concerted diplomatic positions. The Atlantic Community grows, not like a volcanic mountain, by one mighty explosion, but like a coral reef, from the accumulating activity of all.

Thus, we in the free world are moving steadily toward unity and cooperation, in the teeth of that old Bolshevik prophecy, and at the very time when extraordinary rumbles of discord can be heard across the Iron Curtain. It is not free societites which bear within them the seeds of inevitable disunity.

X. OUR BALANCE OF PAYMENTS

On one special problem, of great concern to our friends, and to us, I am proud to give the Congress an encouraging report. Our efforts to safeguard the dollar are progressing. In the 11 months preceding last February 1, we suffered a net loss of nearly $2 billion in gold. In the 11 months that followed, the loss was just over half a billion dollars. And our deficit in our basic transactions with the rest of the world — trade, defense, foreign aid, and capital, excluding volatile short-term flows — has been reduced from $2 billion for 1960 to about one-third that amount for 1961. Speculative fever against the dollar is ending — and confidence in the dollar has been restored.

We did not — and could not — achieve these gains through import restrictions, troop withdrawals, exchange controls, dollar devaluation or choking off domestic recovery. We acted not in panic but in perspective. But the problem is not yet solved. Persistently large deficits would endanger our economic growth and our military and defense commitments abroad. Our goal must be a reasonable equilibrium in our balance of payments. With the cooperation of the Congress, business, labor, and our major allies. that goal can be reached.

We shall continue to attract foreign tourists and investments to our shores, to seek increased military purchases here by our allies, to maximize foreign aid procurement from American firms, to urge increased aid from other fortunate nations to the less fortunate, to seek tax laws which do not favor investment in other industrialized nations or tax havens, and to urge coordination of allied fiscal and monetary policies so as to discourage large and disturbing capital movements.

TRADE

Above all, if we are to pay for our commitments abroad, we must expand our exports. Our businessmen must be export-conscious and export competitive. Our tax policies must spur modernization of our plants – our wage and price gains must be consistent with productivity to hold the line on prices –our export credit and promotion campaigns for American industries must continue to expand.

But the greatest challenge of all is posed by the growth of the European Common Market. Assuming the accession of the United Kingdom, there will arise across the Atlantic a trading partner behind a single external tariff similar to ours with an economy which nearly equals our own. Will we in this country adapt our thinking to these new prospects and patterns or will we wait until events have passed us by?

This is the year to decide. The Reciprocal Trade Act is expiring. We need a new law – a wholly new appraoch – a bold new instrument of American trade policy. Our decision could well affect the unity of the West, the course of the Cold War, and the economic growth of our Nation for a generation to come. . . .

Members of the Congress: The United States did not rise to greatness by waiting for others to lead. This Nation is the world's foremost manufacturer, farmer, banker, consumer, and exporter. The Common Market is moving ahead at an economic growth rate twice ours. The Communist economic offensive is under way. The opportunity is ours – the initiative is up to us – and I believe that 1962 is the time.

To seize that initiative, I shall shortly send to the Congress a new five-year Trade Expansion Action, far-reaching in scope but designed with great care to make certain that its benefits to our people far outweigh any risks. The bill will permit the gradual elimination of tariffs here in the United States and in the Common Market on those items in which we together supply 80 percent of the world's trade – mostly items in which our own ability to compete is demonstrated by the fact that we sell abroad, in these items, substantially more than we import. This step will make it possible for our major industries to compete with their counterparts in Western Europe for access to European consumers.

On other goods the bill will permit a gradual reduction of duties up to 50 percent – permitting bargaining by major categories – and provide for appropriate and tested forms of assistance to firms and employees adjusting to import competition. We are not neglecting the safeguards provided by peril points, an escape clause, or the National Security Amendment. Nor are we abandoning our non-European friends or our traditional "most-favored nation" principle. On the contrary, the bill will provide new encouragement for their sale of tropical agricultural products, so important to our friends in Latin America, who have long depended upon the European Market, who now find themselves faced with new challenges which we must join with them in overcoming. . . .

These various elements in our foreign policy lead, as I have said, to a single goal — the goal of a peaceful world of free and independent states. This is our guide for the present and our vision for the future — a free community of nations, independent but interdependent, uniting north and south, east and west, in one great family of man, outgrowing and transcending the hates and fears that rend our age. . . .

A year ago, in assuming the tasks of the Presidency, I said that few generations, in all history, had been granted the role of being the great defender of freedom in its hour of maximum danger. This is our good fortune; and I welcome it now as I did a year ago. For it is the fate of this generation—of you in the Congress and of me as President — to live with a struggle we did not start, in a world we did not make. But the pressures of life are not always distributed by choice. And while no nation has ever faced such a challenge, no nation has ever been so ready to seize the burden and the glory of freedom.

And in this high endeavor, may God watch over the United States of America.

SPEECH ON THE CUBAN MISSILE CRISIS
October 22, 1962

*Probably no incident or crisis in the history of the Cold
War was more fraught with danger than the confrontation
between Russia and the United States in October, 1962.
In an atmosphere filled with fear and anxiety, the President made a television and radio address to the American people explaining the issues at stake and the policies he had chosen to follow.*

This Government, as promised, has maintained the closest surveillance of the Soviet military buildup on the island of Cuba. Within the
past week, unmistakable evidence has established the fact that a series
of offensive missile sites is now in preparation on that imprisoned island. The purpose of these bases can be none other than to provide a
nuclear strike capability against the Western Hemisphere.

Upon receiving the first preliminary hard information of this nature last Tuesday morning at 9 a.m., I directed that our surveillance
be stepped up. And having now confirmed and completed our evaluation of the evidence and our decision on a course of action, this Government feels obliged to report this new crisis to you in fullest detail.

The characteristics of these new missile sites indicate two dis-
tinct types of installations. Several of them include medium range
ballistic missiles, capable of carrying a nuclear warhead for a dis-
tance of more than 1,000 nautical miles. Each of these missiles, in
short, is capable of striking Washington, D.C., the Panama Canal,
Cape Canaveral, Mexico City, or any other city in the southeastern
part of the United States, in Central America, or in the Caribbean
area.

Additional sites not yet completed appear to be designed for inter-
mediate range ballistic missiles —capable of traveling more than twice
as far — and thus capable of striking most of the major cities in the
Western Hemisphere, ranging as far north as Hudson Bay, Canada,
and as far south as Lima, Peru. In addition, jet bombers, capable of
carrying nuclear weapons, are now being uncrated and assembled in
Cuba, while the necessary air bases are being prepared.

This urgent transformation of Cuba into an important strategic
base — by the presence of these large, long-range, and clearly offensive weapons of sudden mass destruction — constitutes an explicit
threat to the peace and security of all the Americas, in flagrant and
deliberate defiance of the Rio Pact of 1947, the traditions of this
Nation and hemisphere, the joint resolution of the 87th Congress, the
Charter of the United Nations, and my own public warnings to the

will be justified. I have directed the Armed Forces to prepare for any eventualities; and I trust that in the interest of both the Cuban people and the Soviet technicians at the sites, the hazards to all concerned of continuing this threat will be recognized.

Third: It shall be the policy of this Nation to regard any nuclear missile launched from Cuba against any nation in the Western Hemisphere as an attack by the Soviet Union on the United States, requiring a full retaliation response upon the Soviet Union.

Fourth: As a necessary military precaution, I have reinforced our base at Guantanamo, evacuated today the dependents of our personnel there, and ordered additional military units to be on a standby alert basis.

Fifth: We are calling tonight for an immediate meeting of the Organ of Consultation under the Organization of American States, to consider this threat to hemispheric security and to invoke articles 6 and 8 of the Rio Treaty in support of all necessary action. The United Nations Charter allows for regional security arrangements — and the nations of this hemisphere decided long ago against the military presence of outside powers. Our other allies around the world have also been alerted.

Sixth: Under the Charter of the United Nations, we are asking tonight that an emergency meeting of the Security Council be convoked without delay to take action against this latest Soviet threat to world peace. Our resolution will call for the prompt dismantling and withdrawal of all offensive weapons in Cuba, under the supervision of U.N. observers, before the quarantine can be lifted.

Seventh and finally: I call upon Chairman Khrushchev to halt and eliminate this clandestine, reckless, and provocative threat to world peace and to stable relations between our two nations. I call upon him further to abandon this course of world domination, and to join in an historic effort to end the perilous arms race and to transform the history of man. He has an opportunity now to move the world back from the abyss of destruction — by returning to his government's own words that it had no need to station missiles outside its own territory, and withdrawing these weapons from Cuba — by refraining from any action which will widen or deepen the present crisis — and then by participating in a search for peaceful and permanent solutions.

This Nation is prepared to present its case against the Soviet threat to peace, and our own proposals for a peaceful world, at any time and in any forum — in the OAS, in the United Nations, or in any other meeting that could be useful — without limiting our freedom of action. We have in the past made strenuous efforts to limit the spread of nuclear weapons. We have proposed the elimination of all arms and military bases in a fair and effective disarmament treaty. We are prepared to discuss new proposals for the removal of tensions on both sides — including the possibilities of a genuinely independent Cuba, free to determine its own destiny. We have no wish to war with the Soviet Union — for we are a peaceful people who desire to live in peace with all other peoples.

But it is difficult to settle or even discuss these problems in an atmosphere of intimidation. That is why this latest Soviet threat — or any other threat which is made either independently or in response to our actions this week — must and will be met with determination. Any hostile move anywhere in the world against the safety and freedom of peoples to whom we are committed — including in particular the brave people of West Berlin — will be met by whatever action is needed.

Finally, I want to say a few words to the captive people of Cuba, to whom this speech is being directly carried by special radio facilities. I speak to you as a friend, as one who knows of your deep attachment to your fatherland, as one who shares your aspirations for liberty and justice for all. And I have watched and the American people have watched with deep sorrow how your nationalist revolution was betrayed — and how your fatherland fell under foreign domination. Now your leaders are no longer Cuban leaders inspired by Cuban ideals. They are puppets and agents of an international conspiracy which has turned Cuba against your friends and neighbors in the Americas — and turned it into the first Latin American country to become a target for nuclear war — the first Latin American country to have these weapons on its soil.

These new weapons are not in your interest. They contribute nothing to your peace and well-being. They can only undermine it. But this country has no wish to cause you to suffer or to impose any system upon you. We know that your lives and land are being used as pawns by those who deny your freedom.

Many times in the past, the Cuban people have risen to throw out tyrants who destroyed their liberty. And I have no doubt that most Cubans today look forward to the time when they will be truly free — free from foreign domination, free to choose their own leaders, free to select their own system, free to own their own land, free to speak and write and worship without fear or degradation. And then shall Cuba be welcomed back to the society of free nations and to the assocations of this hemisphere.

My fellow citizens: let no one doubt that this is a difficult and dangerous effort on which we have set out. No one can foresee precisely what course it will take or what costs or casualties will be incurred. Many months of sacrifice and self-discipline lie ahead — months in which both our patience and our will will be tested — months in which many threats and denunciations will keep us aware of our dangers. But the greatest danger of all would be to do nothing.

The path we have chosen for the present is full of hazards, as all paths are — but it is the one most consistent with our character and courage as a nation and our commitments around the world. The cost of freedom is always high — but Americans have always paid it. And one path we shall never choose, and that is the path of surrender or submission.

Our goal is not the victory of might, but the vindication of right — not peace at the expense of freedom, but both peace and freedom, here in this hemisphere, and, we hope, around the world. God willing, that goal will be achieved.

Thank you and good night.

THIRD ANNUAL MESSAGE TO CONGRESS
January 14, 1963

*Kennedy's first Congress, the Eighty-seventh, had failed
to pass some of the key measures in his legislative program. Those bills that did pass were often watered-
down versions of what he had requested. He spoke now
to a new Congress, the Eighty-eighth, in a mood of
hopefulness. The Democrats retained large majorities in
both Houses of Congress, but the Southern Democrat-
conservative Republican coalition also remained intact.*

I congratulate you all — not merely on your electoral victory but
on your selected role in history. For you and I are privileged to serve
the great Republic in what could be the most decisive decade in its
long history. The choices we make, for good or ill, may well shape the
state of the Union for generations yet to come.

Little more than 100 weeks ago I assumed the office of President
of the United States. In seeking the help of the Congress and our
countrymen, I pledged no easy answers. I pledged — and asked — only
toil and dedication. These the Congress and the people have given in
good measure. And today, having witnessed in recent months a heightened respect for our national purpose and power — having seen the
courageous calm of a united people in a perilous hour — and having
observed a steady improvement in the opportunities and well-being of
our citizens — I can report to you that the state of this old but youthful
Union, in the 175th year of its life, is good.

In the world beyond our borders, steady progress has been made in
building a world of order. The people of West Berlin remain both free
and secure. A settlement, though still precarious, has been reached
in Laos. The spearpoint of aggression has been blunted in Viet-Nam.
The end of agony may be in sight in the Congo. The doctrine of troika
is dead. And, while danger continues, a deadly threat has been re-
moved in Cuba.

At home, the recession is behind us. Well over a million more men
and women are working today than were working 2 years ago. The
average factory workweek is once again more than 40 hours; our industries are turning out more goods than ever before; and more than
half of the manufacturing capacity that lay silent and wasted 100 weeks
ago is humming with activity.

In short, both at home and abroad, there may now be a temptation
to relax. For the road has been long, the burden heavy, and the pace
consistently urgent.

But we cannot be satisfied to rest here. This is the side of the hill, not the top. The mere absence of war is not peace. The mere absence of recession is not growth. We have made a beginning – but we have only begun.

Now the time has come to make the most of our gains – to translate the renewal of our national strength into the achievement of our national purpose.

II

America has enjoyed 22 months of uninterrupted economic recovery. But recovery is not enough. If we are to prevail in the long run, we must expand the long-run strength of our economy. We must move along the path to a higher rate of growth and full employment.

For this would mean tens of billions of dollars more each year in production, profits, wages, and public revenues. It would mean an end to the persistent slack which has kept our unemployment at or above 5 percent for 61 out of the past 62 months – and an end of the growing pressures for such restrictive measures as the 35-hour week, which alone could increase hourly labor costs by as much as 14 percent, start a new wage-price spiral of inflation, and undercut our efforts to compete with other nations.

To achieve these greater gains, one step, above all, is essential – the enactment this year of a substantial reduction and revision in Federal income taxes.

For it is increasingly clear – to those in Government, business, and labor who are responsible for our economy's success – that our obsolete tax system exerts too heavy a drag on private purchasing power, profits, and employment. Designed to check inflation in earlier years, it now checks growth instead. It discourages extra effort and risk. It distorts the use of resources. It invites recurrent recessions, depresses our Federal revenues, and causes chronic budget deficits.

Now, when the inflationary pressures of the war and the post-war years no longer threaten, and the dollar commands new respect – now, when no military crisis strains our resources – now is the time to act. We cannot afford to be timid or slow. For this is the most urgent task confronting the Congress in 1963.

In an early message, I shall propose a permanent reduction in tax rates which will lower liabilities by $13.5 billion. Of this, $11 billion results from reducing individual tax rates, which now range between 20 and 91 percent, to a more sensible range of 14 to 65 percent, with a split in the present first bracket. Two and one-half billion dollars results from reducing corporate tax rates, from 52 percent – which gives the Government today a majority interest in profits – to the permanent pre-Korean level of 47 percent. This is in addition to the more than $2 billion cut in corporate tax liabilities resulting from last year's investment credit and depreciation reform.

To achieve this reduction within the limits of a manageable budgetary deficit, I urge: first, that these cuts be phased over 3 calendar years, beginning in 1963 with a cut of some $6 billion at annual rates; second, that these reductions be coupled with selected structural changes, beginning in 1964, which will broaden the tax base, end unfair or unnecessary preferences, remove or lighten certain hardships, and in the net offset some $3.5 billion of the revenue loss; and third, that budgetary receipts at the outset be increased by $1.5 billion a year, without any change in tax liabilities, by gradually shifting the tax payments of large corporations to a more current time schedule. This combined program, by increasing the amount of our national income, will in time result in still higher Federal revenues. It is a fiscally responsible program − the surest and the soundest way of achieving in time a balanced budget in a balanced full employment economy,

This net reduction in tax liabilities of $10 billion will increase the purchasing power of American families and business enterprises in every tax bracket, with greatest increase going to our low-income consumers. It will, in addition, encourage the initiative and risk-taking on which our free system depends–induce more investment, production, and capacity use–help provide the 2 million new jobs we need every year– and reinforce the American principle of additional reward for additional effort.

I do not say that a measure for tax reduction and reform is the only way to achieve these goals.

− No doubt a massive increase in Federal spending could also create jobs and growth − but, in today's setting, private consumers, employers, and investors should be given a full opportunity first.

− No doubt a temporary tax cut could provide a spur to our economy − but a long-run problem compels a long-run solution.

− No doubt a reduction in either individual or corporation taxes alone would be of great help − but corporations need customers and job seekers need jobs.

− No doubt tax reduction without reform would sound simpler and more attractive to many − but our growth is also hampered by a host of tax inequities and special preferences which have distorted the flow of investment.

− And, finally, there are no doubt some who would prefer to put off a tax cut in the hope that ultimately an end to the cold war would make possible an equivalent cut in expenditures − but that end is not in view and to wait for it would be costly and self-defeating.

In submitting a tax program which will, of course, temporarily increase the deficit but can ultimately end it − and in recognition of the

need to control expenditures – I will shortly submit a fiscal 1964 administrative budget which, while allowing for needed rises in defense,
space, and fixed interest charges, holds total expenditures for all other
purposes below this year's level.

This requires the reduction or postponement of many desirable
programs, the absorption of a large part of last year's Federal pay
raise through personnel and other economies, the termination of certain installations and projects, and the substitution in several programs
of private for public credit. But I am convinced that the enactment this
year of tax reduction and tax reform overshadows all other domestic
problems in this Congress. For we cannot for long lead the cause of
peace and freedom, if we ever cease to set the pace here at home.

III

Tax reduction alone, however, is not enough to strengthen our
society, to provide opportunities for the four million Americans who
are born every year, to improve the lives of 32 million Americans
who live on the outskirts of poverty.

The quality of American life must keep pace with the quantity of
American goods.

This country cannot afford to be materially rich and spiritually
poor.

Therefore, by holding down the budgetary cost of existing programs
to keep within the limitations I have set, it is both possible and im-
perative to adopt other new measures that we cannot afford to postpone.

These measures are based on a series of fundamental premises,
grouped under four related headings:

First, we need to strengthen our Nation by investing in our youth:

–The future of any country which is dependent upon the will and
wisdom of its citizens is damaged, and irreparably damaged, whenever
any of its children is not educated to the full extent of his talent, from
grade school through graduate school. Today, an estimated 4 out of
every 10 students in the 5th grade will not even finish high school –
and that is a waste we cannot afford.

–In addition, there is no reason why one million young Americans,
out of school and out of work, should all remain unwanted and often
untrained on our city streets when their energies can be put to good use.

–Finally, the overseas success of our Peace Corps volunteers,
most of them young men and women carrying skills and ideas to needy
people, suggests the merit of a similar corps serving our own community needs: in mental hospitals, on Indian reservations, in centers
for the aged or for young delinquents, in schools for the illiterate or

the handicapped. As the idealism of our youth has served world peace, so can it serve the domestic tranquility.

Second, we need to strengthen our Nation by safeguarding its health:

—Our working men and women, instead of being forced to beg for help from public charity once they are old and ill, should start contributing now to their own retirement health program through the Social Security System.

—Moreover, all our miracles of medical research will count for little if we cannot reverse the growing nationwide shortage of doctors, dentists, and nurses, and the widespread shortages of nursing homes and modern urban hospital facilities. Merely to keep the present ratio of doctors and dentists from declining any further, we must over the next 10 years increase the capacity of our medical schools by 50 percent and our dental schools by 100 percent.

—Finally, and of deep concern, I believe that the abandonment of the mentally ill and the mentally retarded to the grim mercy of custodial institutions too often inflicts on them and on their families a needless cruelty which this Nation should not endure. The incidence of mental retardation in this country is three times as high as that of Sweden, for example — and that figure can and must be reduced.

Third, we need to strengthen our Nation by protecting the basic rights of its citizens:

—The right to competent counsel must be assured to every man accused of crime in Federal court, regardless of his means.

—And the most precious and powerful right in the world, the right to vote in a free American election, must not be denied to any citizen on grounds of his race or color. I wish that all qualified Americans permitted to vote were willing to vote, but surely in this centennial year of Emancipation all those who are willing to vote should always be permitted.

Fourth, we need to strengthen our Nation by making the best and the most economical use of its resources and facilities:

—Our economic health depends on healthy transportation arteries; and I believe the way to a more modern, economical choice of national transportation service is through increased competition and decreased regulation. Local mass transit, faring even worse, is as essential a community service as hospitals and highways. Nearly three-fourths of our citizens live in urban areas, which occupy only 2 percent of our land — and if local transit is to survive and relieve the congestion of these cities, it needs Federal stimulation and assistance.

—Next, this Government is in the storage and stockpile business to the melancholy tune of more than $16 billion. We must continue to support farm income, but we should not pile more farm surpluses on top of the $7.5 billion we already own. We must maintain a stockpile of strategic materials but the $8.5 billion we have acquired — for reasons both good and bad — is much more than we need; and we should be empowered to dispose of the excess in ways which will not cause market disruption.

—Finally, our already overcrowded national parks and recreation areas will have twice as many visitors 10 years from now as they do today. If we do not plan today for the future growth of these and other great natural assets — not only parks and forests but wildlife and wilderness preserves, and water project of all kinds — our children and their children will be poorer in every sense of the word.

These are not domestic concerns alone. For upon our achievement of greater vitality and strength here at home hang our fate and future in the world: our ability to sustain and supply the security of free men and nations, our ability to command their respect for our leadership, our ability to expand our trade without threat to our balance of payments, and our ability to adjust to the changing demands of cold war competition and challenge.

We shall be judged more by what we do at home than by what we preach abroad. Nothing we could do to help the developing countries would help them half as much as a booming U.S. economy. And nothing our opponents could do to encourage their own ambitions would encourage them half as much as a chronic lagging U.S. economy. These domestic tasks do not divert energy from our security — they provide the very foundation for freedom's survival and success.

IV

Turning to the world outside, it was only a few years ago — in Southeast Asia, Africa, Eastern Europe, Latin America, even outer space — that communism sought to convey the image of a unified, confident, and expanding empire, closing in on a sluggish America and a free world in disarray. But few people would hold to that picture today.

In these past months we have reaffirmed the scientific and military superiority of freedom. We have doubled our efforts in space, to assure us of being first in the future. We have undertaken the most far-reaching defense improvements in the peacetime history of this country. And we have maintained the frontiers of freedom from Viet-Nam to West Berlin.

But complacency or self-congratulation can imperil our security as much as the weapons of tyranny. A moment of pause is not a promise of peace. Dangerous problems remain from Cuba to the South China Sea. The world's prognosis prescribes, in short, not a year's vacation for us, but a year of obligation and opportunity.

Four special avenues of opportunity stand out: the Atlantic Alliance, the developing nations, the new Sino-Soviet difficulties, and the search for worldwide peace.

V

First, how fares the grand alliance? Free Europe is entering into a new phase of its long and brilliant history. The era of colonial expansion has passed; the era of national rivalries is fading; and a new era of interdependence and unity is taking shape. Defying the old prophecies of Marx, consenting to what no conqueror could ever compel, the free nations of Europe are moving toward a unity of purpose and power and policy in every sphere of activity.

For 17 years this movement has had our consistent support, both political and economic. Far from resenting the new Europe, we regard her as a welcome partner, not a rival. For the road to world peace and freedom is still long, and there are burdens which only full partners can share — in supporting the common defense, in expanding world trade, in aligning our balance of payments, in aiding the emergent nations, in concerting political and economic policies, and in welcoming to our common effort other industrialized nations, notably Japan, whose remarkable economic and political development of the 1950's permits it now to play on the world scene a major constructive role.

No doubt differences of opinion will continue to get more attention than agreements on action, as Europe moves from independence to more formal interdependence. But these are honest differences among honorable associates — more real and frequent, in fact, among our Western European allies than between them and the United States. For the unity of freedom has never relied on uniformity of opinion. But the basic agreement of this alliance on fundamental issues continues.

The first task of the alliance remains the common defense. Last month Prime Minister Macmillan and I laid plans for a new stage in our long cooperative effort, one which aims to assist in the wider task of framing a common nuclear defense for the whole alliance.

The Nassau agreement recognizes that the security of the West is indivisible, and so must be our defense. But it also recognizes that this is an alliance of proud and sovereign nations, and works best when we do not forget it. It recognizes further that the nuclear defense of the West is not a matter for the present nuclear powers alone — that France will be such a power in the future — and that ways must be found without increasing the role of our other partners in planning, manning, and directing a truly multilateral nuclear force within an increasingly intimate NATO alliance. Finally, the Nassau agreement recognizes that nuclear defense is not enough, that the agreed NATO levels of conventional strength must be met, and that the alliance cannot afford to be in a position of having to answer every threat with nuclear weapons or nothing.

We remain too near the Nassau decisions, and too far from their full realization, to know their place in history. But I believe that, for the first time, the door is open for the nuclear defense of the alliance to become a source of confidence, instead of a cause of contention.

The next most pressing concern of the alliance is our common economic goals of trade and growth. This Nation continues to be concerned about its balance-of-payments deficit, which, despite its decline, remains a stubborn and troublesome problem. We believe, moreover, that closer economic ties among all free nations are essential to prosperity and peace. And neither we nor the members of the European Common Market are so affluent that we can long afford to shelter high cost farms or factories from the winds of foreign competition, or to restrict the channels of trade with other nations of the free world. If the Common Market should move toward protectionism and restrictionism, it would undermine its own basic principles. This Government means to use the authority conferred on it last year by the Congress to encourage trade expansion on both sides of the Atlantic and around the world.

VI

Second, what of the developing and non-aligned nations? They were shocked by the Soviets' sudden and secret attempt to transform Cuba into a nuclear striking base — and by Communist China's arrogant invasion of India. They have been reassured by our prompt assistance to India, by our support through the United Nations of the Congo's unification, by our patient search for disarmament, and by the improvement in our treatment of citizens and visitors whose skins do not happen to be white. And as the older colonialism recedes, and the neo-colonialism of the Communist powers stands out more starkly than ever, they realize more clearly that the issue in the world struggle is not, communism versus capitalism, but coercion versus free choice.

They are beginning to realize that the longing for independence is the same the world over, whether it is the independence of West Berlin or Viet-Nam. They are beginning to realize that such independence runs athwart all Communist ambitions but is in keeping with our own — and that our approach to their diverse needs is resilient and resourceful, while the Communists are still relying on ancient doctrines and dogmas.

Nevertheless it is hard for any nation to focus on an external or subversive threat to its independence when its energies are drained in daily combat with the forces of poverty and despair. It makes little sense for us to assail, in speeches and resolutions, the horrors of communism, to spend $50 billion a year to prevent its military advance — and then to begrudge spending, largely on American products, less than one-tenth of that amount to help other nations strengthen their independence and cure the social chaos in which communism always has thrived.

I am proud — and I think most Americans are proud — of a mutual defense and assistance program, evolved with bipartisan support in three administrations, which has, with all its recognized problems, contributed to the fact that not a single one of the nearly fifty U.N. members to gain independence since the Second World War has succumbed to Communist control.

I am proud of a program that has helped to arm and feed and clothe millions of people who live on the front lines of freedom.

I am especially proud that this country has put forward for the 60's a vast cooperative effort to achieve economic growth and social progress throughout the Americas — the Alliance for Progress.

I do not underestimate the difficulties that we face in this mutual effort among our close neighbors, but the free states of this hemisphere, working in close collaboration, have begun to make this alliance a living reality. Today it is feeding one out of every four school age children in Latin America an extra food ration from our farm surplus. It has distributed 1.5 million school books and is building 17,000 classrooms. It has helped resettle tens of thousands of farm families on land they can call their own. It is stimulating our good neighbors to more self-help and self-reform — fiscal, social, institutional, and land reforms. It is bringing new housing and hope, new health and dignity, to millions who were forgotten. The men and women of this hemisphere know that the alliance cannot succeed if it is only another name for United States handouts — that it can succeed only as the Latin American nations themselves devote their best effort to fulfilling its goals.

This story is the same in Africa, in the Middle East, and in Asia. Wherever nations are willing to help themselves, we stand ready to help them build new bulwarks of freedom. We are not purchasing votes for the cold war; we have gone to the aid of imperiled nations, neutrals and allies alike. What we do ask — and all that we ask — is that our help be used to best advantage, and that their own efforts not be diverted by needless quarrels with other independent nations.

Despite all its past achievements, the continued progress of the mutual assistance program requires a persistent discontent with present performance. We have been reorganizing this program to make it a more effective, efficient instrument – and that process will continue this year.

But free world development will still be an uphill struggle. Government aid can only supplement the role of private investment, trade expansion, commodity stabilization, and, above all, internal self-improvement. The processes of growth are gradual—bearing fruit in a decade, not a day. Our successes will be neither quick nor dramatic. But if these programs were ever to be ended, our failures in a dozen countries would be sudden and certain.

Neither money nor technical assistance, however, can be our only weapon against poverty. In the end, the crucial effort is one of purpose, requiring the fuel of finance but also a torch of idealism. And nothing carries the spirit of this American idealism more effectively to the far corners of the earth than the American Peace Corps.

A year ago, less than 900 Peace Corps volunteers were on the job. A year from now they will number more than 9,000 – men and women, aged 18 to 79, willing to give 2 years of their lives to helping people in other lands.

There are, in fact, nearly a million Americans serving their country and the cause of freedom in overseas posts, a record no other people can match. Surely those of us who stay at home should be glad to help indirectly; by supporting our aid programs; by opening our doors to foreign visitors and diplomats and students; and by proving, day by day, by deed as well as word, that we are a just and generous people.

VII

Third, what comfort can we take from the increasing strains and tensions within the Communist bloc? Here hope must be tempered with caution. For the Soviet-Chinese disagreement is over means, not ends. A dispute over how best to bury the free world is no grounds for Western rejoicing.

Nevertheless, while a strain is not a fracture, it is clear that the forces of diversity are at work inside the Communist camp, despite all the iron disciplines of regimentation and all the iron dogmatisms of ideology. Marx is proven wrong once again: for it is the closed Communist societies, not the free and open societies which carry within themselves the seeds of internal disintegration.

The disarray of the Communist empire has been heightened by two other formidable forces. One is the historical force of nationalism – and the yearning of all men to be free. The other is the gross inefficiency of their economies. For a closed society is not open to ideas of progress – and a police state finds that it cannot command the grain to grow.

New nations asked to choose between two competing systems need only compare conditions in East and West Germany, Eastern and Western Europe, North and South Viet-Nam. They need only compare the disillusionment of Communist Cuba with the promise of the Alliance for Progress. And all the world knows that no successful system builds a wall to keep its people in and freedom out — and the wall of shame dividing Berlin is a symbol of Communist failure.

VIII

Finally, what can we do to move from the present pause toward enduring peace? Again I would counsel catuion. I foresee no spectacular reversal in Communist methods or goals. But if all these trends and developments can persuade the Soviet Union to walk the path of peace, then let her know that all free nations will journey with her. But until that choice is made, and until the world can develop a reliable system of international security, the free peoples have no choice but to keep their arms nearby.

This country, therefore, continues to require the best defense in the world — a defense which is suited to the sixties. This means, unfortunately, a rising defense budget — for there is no substitute for adequate defense, and no "bargain basement" way of achieving it. It means the expenditure of more than $15 billion this year on nuclear weapons systems alone, a sum which is about equal to the combined defense budgets of our European Allies.

But it also means improved air and missile defenses, improved civil defense, a strengthened anti-guerrilla capacity and, of prime importance, more powerful and flexible non-nuclear forces. For threats of massive retaliation may not deter piecemeal aggression — and a line of destroyers in a quarantine, or a division of well-equipped men on a border, may be more useful to our real security than the multiplication of awesome weapons beyond all rational need.

But our commitment to national safety is not a commitment to expand our military establishment indefinitely. We do not dismiss disarmament as merely an idle dream. For we believe that, in the end, it is the only way to assure the security of all without impairing the interests of any. Nor do we mistake honorable negotiation for appeasement. While we shall never weary in the defense of freedom, neither shall we ever abandon the pursuit of peace.

In this quest, the United Nations requires our full and continued support. Its value in serving the cause of peace has been shown anew in its role in the West New Guinea settlement, in its use as a forum for the Cuban crisis, and in its task of unification in the Congo. Today the United Nations is primarily the protector of the small and the weak, and a safety valve for the strong. Tomorrow it can form the framework for

a world of law — a world in which no nation dictates the destiny of another, and in which the vast resources now devoted to destructive
means will serve constructive ends.

In short, let our adversaries choose. If they choose peaceful competition, they shall have it. If they come to realize that their ambitions
cannot succeed — if they see their "wars of liberation" and subversion
will ultimately fail — if they recognize that there is more security in
accepting inspection than in permitting new nations to master the
black arts of nuclear war — and if they are willing to turn their energies, as we are, to the great unfinished tasks of our own peoples —
than, surely, the areas of agreement can be very wide indeed: a clear
understanding about Berlin, stability in Southeast Asia, an end to
nuclear testing, new checks on surprise or accidental attack, and, ultimately, general and complete disarmament.

IX

For we seek not the worldwide victory of one nation or system but
a worldwide victory of man. The modern globe is too small, its weapons are too destructive, and its disorders are too contagious to permit any other kind of victory.

To achieve this end, the United States will continue to spend a
greater portion of its national production than any other people in the
free world. For 15 years no other free nation has demanded so much
of itself. Through hot wars and cold, through recession and prosperity,
through the ages of the atom and outer space, the American people
have never faltered and their faith has never flagged. If at times our
actions seem to make life difficult for others, it is only because history has made life difficult for us all.

But difficult days need not be dark. I think these are proud and
memorable days in the cause of peace and freedom. We are proud, for
example, of Major Rudolf Anderson who gave his life over the island
of Cuba. We salute Specialist James Allen Johnson who died on the
border of South Korea. We pay honor to Sergeant Gerald Pendell who
was killed in Viet-Nam. They are among the many who in this century,
far from home, have died for our country. Our task now, and the task
of all Americans is to live up to their commitment.

My friends: I close on a note of hope. We are not lulled by the
momentary calm of the sea or the somewhat clearer skies above. We
know the turbulence that lies below, and the storms that are beyond the
horizon this year. But now the winds of change appear to be blowing
more strongly than ever, in the world of communism as well as our
own. For 175 years we have sailed with those winds at our back, and
with the tides of human freedom in our favor. We steer our ship with
hope, as Thomas Jefferson said, "Leaving Fear astern."

ADDRESS ON WORLD PEACE
Commencement Address at American University
June 10, 1963

*This speech, acknowledged by most observers to have
been one of Kennedy's finest, displayed a more generous attitude toward the Soviet Union than was present
in most of his speeches. The President's tone was pos-
tive and hopeful about improved relations between the
two countries. He called for a reexamination of American as well as Soviet attitudes toward the problems dividing them, and he stressed the enormous cost of military spending at the expense of sorely needed domestic
reforms.*

I have . . . chosen this time and this place to discuss a topic on
which ignorance too often abounds and the truth is too rarely per-
ceived — yet it is the most important topic on earth: world peace.

What kind of peace do I mean? What kind of peace do we seek? Not
a Pax Americana enforced on the world by American weapons of war.
Not the peace of the grave or the security of the slave. I am talking
about genuine peace, the kind of peace that makes life on earth worth
living, the kind that enables men and nations to grow and to hope and
to build a better life for their children — not merely peace for Americans but peace for all men and women — not merely peace in our time
but peace for all time.

I speak of peace because of the new face of war. Total war makes
no sense in an age when great powers can maintain large and relatively
invulnerable nuclear forces and refuse to surrender without resort to
those forces. It makes no sense in an age when a single nuclear weapon
contains almost ten times the explosive force delivered by all of the
allied air forces in the Second World War. It makes no sense in an age
when the deadly poisons produced by a nuclear exchange would be carried by wind and water and soil and seed to the far corners of the
globe and to generations yet unborn.

Today the expenditure of billions of dollars every year on weapons
acquired for the purpose of making sure we never need to use them is
essential to keeping the peace. But surely the acquisition of such idle
stockpiles — which can only destroy and never create — is not the only,
much less the most efficient, means of assuring peace.

I speak of peace, therefore, as the necessary rational end of rational
men. I realize that the pursuit of peace is not as dramatic as the pursuit of war — and frequently the words of the pursuer fall on deaf ears.
But we have no more urgent task.

Today we still welcome those winds of change— and we hav
reason to believe that our tide is running strong. With thanks
mighty God for seeing us through a perilous passage, we ask H
anew in guiding the "Good Ship Union."

Some say that it is useless to speak of world peace or world law or world disarmament — and that it will be useless until the leaders of the Soviet Union adopt a more enlightened attitude. I hope they do. I believe we can help them do it. But I also believe that we must reexamine our own attitude — as individuals and as a Nation — for our attitude is as essential as theirs. And every graduate of this school, every thoughtful citizen who despairs of war and wishes to bring peace, should begin by looking inward — by examining his own attitude toward the possibilities of peace, toward the Soviet Union, toward the course of the cold war and toward freedom and peace here at home.

First: Let us examine our attitude toward peace itself. Too many of us think it is impossible. Too many think it unreal. But that is a dangerous, defeatist belief. It leads to the conclusion that war is inevitable — that mankind is doomed — that we are gripped by forces we cannot control.

We need not accept that view. Our problems are manmade — therefore, they can be solved by man. And man can be as big as he wants. No problem of human destiny is beyond human beings. Man's reason and spirit have often solved the seemingly unsolvable — and we believe they can do it again.

I am not referring to the absolute, infinite concept of universal peace and good will of which some fantasies and fanatics dream. I do not deny the value of hopes and dreams but we merely invite discouragement and incredulity by making that our only and immediate goal.

Let us focus instead on a more practical, more attainable peace — based not on a sudden revolution in human nature but on a gradual evolution in human institutions — on a series of concrete actions and effective agreements which are in the interest of all concerned. There is no single, simple key to this peace — no grand or magic formula to be adopted by one or two powers. Genuine peace must be the product of many nations, the sum of many acts. It must be dynamic, not static, changing to meet the challenge of each new generation. For peace is a process — a way of solving problems.

With such a peace, there will still be quarrels and conflicting interests, as there are within families and nations. World peace, like community peace, does not require that each man love his neighbor — it requires only that they live together in mutual tolerance, submitting their disputes to a just and peaceful settlement. And history teaches us that enmities between nations, as between individuals, do not last forever. However fixed our likes and dislikes may seem, the tide of time and events will often bring surprising changes in the relations between nations and neighbors.

So let us persevere. Peace need not be impracticable, and war need not be inevitable. By defining our goal more clearly, by making it seem more manageable and less remote, we can help all peoples to see it, to draw hope from it, and to move irresistibly toward it.

Second: Let us reexamine our attitude toward the Soviet Union. It is discouraging to think that their leaders may actually believe what their propagandists write. It is discouraging to read a recent authoritative Soviet text on Military Strategy and find, on page after page, wholly baseless and incredible claims — such as the allegation that "American imperialist circles are preparing to unleash different types of wars. . . that there is a very real threat of a preventive war being unleashed by American imperialists against the Soviet Union . . . and that the political aims of the American imperialists are to enslave economically and politically the European and other capitalist countries . . . and to achieve world domination . . . by means of aggressive wars."

Truly, as it was written long ago: "The wicked flee when no man pursueth." Yet it is sad to read these Soviet statements — to realize the extent of the gulf between us. But it is also a warning — a warning to the American people not to fall into the same trap as the Soviets, not to see only a distorted and desperate view of the other a side, not to see conflict as inevitable, accommodation as impossible, and communication as nothing more than an exchange of threats.

No governments or social system is so evil that its people must be considered as lacking in virtue. As Americans, we find communism profoundly repugnant as a negation of personal freedom and dignity. But we can still hail the Russian people for their many achievements — in science and space, in economic and industrial growth, in culture and in acts of courage.

Among the many traits the peoples of our two countries have in common, none is stronger than our mutual abhorrence of war. Almost unique, among the major world powers, we have never been at war with each other. And no nation in the history of battle ever suffered more that the Soviet Union suffered in the course of the Second World War. At least 20 million lost their lives. Countless millions of homes and farms were burned or sacked. A third of the nation's territory, including nearly two thirds of its industrial base, was turned into a wasteland — a loss equivalent to the devastation of this country east to Chicago.

Today, should total war ever break out again— no matter how — our two countries would become the primary targets It is an ironic but accurate fact that the two strongest powers are the two in the most danger of devastation. All we have built, all we have worked for, would be destroyed in the first 24 hours. And even in the cold war, which brings burdens and dangers to so many countries, including this Nation's closest allies — our two countries bear the heaviest burdens. For we are both devoting massive sums of money to weapons that could be better devoted to combating ignorance, poverty, and disease. We are both caught up in a vicious and dangerous cycle in which suspicion on one side breeds suspicion on the other, and new weapons beget counterweapons.

In short, both the United States and its allies, and the Soviet Union and its allies, have a mutually deep interest in a just and genuine peace and in halting the arms race. Agreements to this end are in the interests of the Soviet Union as well as ours — and even the most hostile nations can be relied upon to accept and keep those treaty obligations, and only those treaty obligations, which are in their own interest.

So, let us not be blind to our differences — but let us also direct attention to our common interests and to the means by which those differences can be resolved. And if we cannot end now our differences, at least we can help make the world safe for diversity. For, in the final analysis, our most basic common link is that we all inhabit this small planet. We all breathe the same air. We all cherish our children's future. And we are all mortal.

Third: Let us reexamine our attitude toward the cold war, remembering that we are not engaged in a debate, seeking to pile up debating points. We are not here distributing blame or pointing the finger of judgment. We must deal with the world as it is, and not as it might have been had the history of the last 18 years been different.

We must, therefore, persevere in the search for peace in the hope that constructive changes within the Communist bloc might bring within reach solutions which now seem beyond us. We must conduct our affairs in such a way that it becomes in the Communists' interest to agree on a genuine peace. Above all, while defending our own vital interests, nuclear powers must avert those confrontations which bring an adversary to a choice of either a humiliating retreat or a nuclear war. To adopt that kind of course in the nuclear age would be evidence only of the bankruptcy of our policy — or of a collective death-wish for the world.

To secure these ends America's weapons are nonprovocative, carefully controlled, designed to deter, and capable of selective use. Our military forces are committed to peace and disciplined in self-restraint. Our diplomats are instructed to avoid unnecessary irritants and purely rhetorical hostility.

For we can seek a relaxation of tensions without relaxing our guard. And, for our part, we do not need to use threats to prove that we are resolute. We do not need to jam foreign broadcasts out of fear our faith will be eroded. We are unwilling to impose our system on any unwilling people — but we are willing and able to engage in peaceful competition with any people on earth.

Meanwhile, we seek to strengthen the United Nations, to help solve its financial problems, to make it a more effective instrument for peace, to develop it into a genuine world security system — a system capable of resolving disputes on the basis of law, of insuring the security of the large and the small, and of creating conditions under which arms can finally be abolished.

At the same time we seek to keep peace inside the non-Communist world, where many nations, all of them our friends, are divided over issues which weaken Western unity, which invite Communist intervention or which threaten to erupt into war. Our efforts in West New Guinea, in the Congo, in the Middle East, and in the Indian subcontinent, have been persistent and patient despite criticism from both sides. We have also tried to set an example for others — by seeking to adjust small but significant differences with our own closest neighbors in Mexico and in Canada.

Speaking of other nations, I wish to make one point clear. We are bound to many nations by alliances. Those alliances exist because our concern and theirs substantially overlap. Our commitment to defend Western Europe and West Berlin, for example, stands undiminished because of the identity of our vital interests. The United States will make no deal with the Soviet Union at the expense of other nations and other peoples, not merely because they are our partners, but also because their interests and ours converge.

Our interests converge, however, not only in defending the frontiers of freedom, but in pursuing the paths of peace. It is our hope — and the purpose of allied policies — to convince the Soviet Union that she, too, should let each nation choose its own future, so long as that choice does not interfere with the choices of others. The Communist drive to impose their political and economic system on others is the primary cause of world tension today. For there can be no doubt that, if all nations could refrain from interfering in the self-determination of others, the peace would be much more assured.

This will require a new effort to achieve world law — a new context for world discussions. It will require increased understanding between the Soviets and ourselves. And increased understanding will require increased contact and communication. One step in this direction is the proposed arrangement for a direct line between Moscow and Washington, to avoid on each side the dangerous delays, misunderstandings, and misreadings of the other's actions which might occur at a time of crisis.

We have also been talking in Geneva about other first-step measures of arms control, designed to limit the intensity of the arms race and to reduce the risks of accidental war. Our primary long-range interest in Geneva, however, is general and complete disarmament — designed to take place by stages, permitting parallel political developments to build the new institutions of peace which would take the place of arms. The pursuit of disarmament has been an effort of this Government since the 1920's. It has been urgently sought by the past three administrations. And however dim the propsects may be today, we intend to continue this effort—to continue it in order that all countries, including our own, can better grasp what the problems and possibilities of disarmament are.

The one major area of these negotiations where the end is in sight, yet where a fresh start is badly needed, is in a treaty to outlaw nuclear tests. The conclusion of such a treaty, so near and yet so far, would check the spiraling arms race in one of its most dangerous areas. It would place the nuclear powers in a position to deal more effectively with one of the greatest hazards which man faces in 1963, the further spread of nuclear arms. It would increase our security – it would decrease the prospects of war. Surely this goal is sufficiently important to require our steady pursuit, yielding neither to the temptation to give up the whole effort nor the temptation to give up our insistence on vital and responsible safeguards.

I am taking this opportunity, therefore, to announce two important decisions in this regard.

First: Chairman Khrushchev, Prime Minister Macmillan, and I have agreed that high-level discussions will shortly begin in Moscow looking toward early agreement on a comprehensive test ban treaty. Our hopes must be tempered with the caution of history – but with our hopes go the hopes of all mankind.

Second: To make clear our good faith and solemn convictions on the matter, I now declare that the United States does not propose to conduct nuclear tests in the atmosphere so long as other states do not do so. We will not be the first to resume. Such a declaration is no substitute for a formal binding treaty, but I hope it will help us achieve one. Nor would such a treaty be a substitute for disarmament, but I hope it will help us achieve it.

Finally, my fellow Americans, let us examine our attitude twoard peace and freedom here at home. The quality and spirit of our own society must justify and support our efforts abroad. We must show it in the dedication of our own lives —as many of you who are graduating today will have a unique opportunity to do, by serving without pay in the Peace Corps abroad or in the proposed National Service Corps here at home.

But wherever we are, we must all, in our daily lives, live up to the age-old faith that peace and freedom walk together. In too many of our cities today, the peace is not secure because freedom is incomplete.

It is the responsibility of the executive branch at all levels of government — local, State, and National — to provide and protect that freedom for all of our citizens by all means within their authority. It is the responsibility of the legislative branch at all levels, wherever that authority is not now adequate, to make it adequate. And it is the responsibility of all citizens in all sections of this country to respect the rights of all others and to respect the law of the land.

All this is not unrelated to world peace. "When a man's ways please the Lord," the Scriptures tell us, "he maketh even his enemies to be at peace with him." And is not peace, in the last analysis, basically a matter of human rights — the right to live out our lives without fear of devastation — the right to breathe air as nature provided it — the right of future generations to a healthy existence?

While we proceed to safeguard our national interests, let us also safeguard human interests. And the elimination of war and arms is clearly in the interest of both. No treaty, however much it may be to the advantage of all, however tightly it may be worded, can provide absolute security against the risks of deception and evasion. But it can — if it is sufficiently effective in its enforcement and if it is sufficiently in the interests of its signers — offer far more security and far fewer risks than an unabated, uncontrolled, unpredictable arms race.

The United States, as the world knows, will never start a war. We do not want a war. We do not now expect a war. This generation of Americans has already had enough — more than enough — of war and hate and oppression. We shall be prepared if others wish it. We shall be alert to try to stop it. But we shall also do our part to build a world of peace where the weak are safe and the strong are just. We are not hopeless before that task or hopeless of its success. Confident and un-afraid, we labor on — not toward a strategy of annihilation but toward a strategy of peace.

CIVIL RIGHTS SPEECH
June 11, 1963

The autumn of 1962 and the first half of 1963 had seen questions of civil rights press inexorably to the fore. In Mississippi, James Merideth had been admitted to the University of Mississippi only after federal marshals and troops had been ordered in by the President. Two persons had been killed and many were injured. In Alabama, two black students had applied for admission to the University of Alabama. The Governor of the state, George Wallace, attempted to block their admission. President Kennedy appeared on nationwide television to explain his responsibilities. The issue was not merely legal — the Governor's action was contrary to court orders — but great moral questions were involved, the President stated.

Good evening, my fellow citizens:

This afternoon, following a series of threats and defiant statements, the presence of Alabama National Guardsmen was required on the University of Alabama [Campus] to carry out the final and unequivocal order of the United States District Court of the Northern District of Alabama. That order called for the admission of two clearly qualified young Alabama residents who happened to have been born Negro.

That they were admitted peacefully on the campus is due in good measure to the conduct of the students of the University of Alabama, who met their responsibilities in a constructive way.

I hope that every American, regardless of where he lives, will stop and examine his conscience about this and other related incidents. This Nation was founded by men of many nations and backgrounds. It was founded on the principle that all men are created equal, and that the rights of every man are diminished when the rights of one man are threatened.

Today we are committed to a worldwide struggle to promote and protect the rights of all who wish to be free. And when Americans are sent to Viet-Nam or West Berlin, we do not ask for whites only. It ought to be possible, therefore, for American students of any color to attend any public institution they select without having to be backed up by troops.

It ought to be possible for American consumers of any color to receive equal service in places of public accommodation, such as hotels and restaurants and theaters and retail stores, without being forced to resort to demonstrations in the street, and it ought to be possible for American citizens of any color to register and to vote in a free election without interference or fear of reprisal.

It ought to be possible, in short, for every American to enjoy the privileges of being American without regard to his race or his color. In short, every American ought to have the right to be treated as he would wish to be treated, as one would wish his children to be treated. But this is not the case.

The Negro baby born in America today, regardless of the section of the Nation is which he is born, had about one-half as much chance of completing a high school as a white baby born in the same place on the same day, one-third as much chance of completing college, one-third as much chance of becoming a professional man, twice as much chance of becoming unemployed, about one-seventh as much chance of earning $10,000 a year, a life expectancy which is 7 years shorter, and the prospects of earning only half as much.

This is not a sectional issue. Difficulties over segregation and discrimination exist in every city, in every State of the Union, producing in many cities a rising tide of discontent that threatens the public safety. Nor is this a partisan issue. In a time of domestic crisis men of good will and generosity should be able to unite regardless of party or politics. This is not even a legal or legislative issue alone. It is better to settle these matters in the courts than on the streets, and new laws are needed at every level, but law alone cannot make men see right.

We are confronted primarily with a moral issue. It is as old as the scriptures and is as clear as the American Constitution.

The heart of the question is whether all Americans are to be afforded equal rights and equal opportunities, whether we are going to treat our fellow Americans as we want to be treated. If an American, because his skin is dark, cannot eat lunch in a restaurant open to the public, if he cannot send his children to the best public school available, if he cannot vote for the public officials who represent him, if, in short, he cannot enjoy the full and free life which all of us want, then who among us would be content to have the color of his skin changed and stand in his place? Who among us would then be content with the counsels of patience and delay?

One hundred years of delay have passed since President Lincoln freed the slaves, yet their heirs, their grandsons, are not fully free. They are not yet freed from the bonds of injustice. They are not yet freed from social and economic oppression. And this Nation, for all its hopes and all its boasts, will not be fully free until all its citizens are free.

We preach freedom around the world, and we mean it, and we cherish our freedom here at home, but are we to say to the world, and much more importantly, to each other that this is a land of the free except for the Negroes; that we have no second-class citizens except Negroes;

that we have no class or caste system, no ghettoes, no master race except with respect to Negroes?

Now the time has come for this Nation to fulfill its promise. The events in Birmingham and elsewhere have so increased the cries for equality that no city or State or legislative body can prudently choose to ignore them.

The fires of frustration and discord are burning in every city, North and South, where legal remedies are not at hand. Redress is sought in the streets, in demonstrations, parades, and protests which create tensions and threaten violence and threaten lives.

We face, therefore, a moral crisis as a country and as a people. It cannot be met by repressive police action. It cannot be left to increased demonstrations in the streets. It cannot be quieted by token moves or talk. It is a time to act in the Congress, in your State and local legislative body and, above all, in all of our daily lives.

It is not enough to pin the blame on others, to say this is a problem of one section of the country or another, or deplore the facts that we face. A great change is at hand, and our task, our obligation, is to make that revolution, that change, peaceful and constructive for all.

Those who do nothing are inviting shame as well as violence. Those who act boldly are recognizing right as well as reality.

Next week I shall ask the Congress of the United States to act, to make a commitment it has not fully made in this century to the proposition that race has no place in American life or law. The Federal judiciary has upheld that proposition in a series of forthright cases. The executive branch has adopted that proposition in the conduct of its affairs, including the employment of Federal personnel, the use of Federal facilities, and the sale of federally financed housing.

But there are other necessary measures which only the Congress can provide, and they must be provided at this session. The old code of equity law under which we live commands for every wrong a remedy, but in too many communities, in too many parts of the country, wrongs are inflicted on Negro citizens and there are no remedies at law. Unless the Congress acts, their only remedy is in the street.

I am, therefore, asking the Congress to enact legislation giving all Americans the right to be served in facilities which are open to the public — hotels, restaurants, theaters, retail stores, and similar establishments.

This seems to me to be an elementary right. Its denial is an arbitrary indignity that no American in 1963 should have to endure, but many do.

I have recently met with scores of business leaders urging them to take voluntary action to end this discrimination and I have been encouraged by their response, and in the last 2 weeks over 75 cities have seen progress made in desegregating these kinds of facilities. But many are unwilling to act alone, and for this reason, nationwide legislation is needed if we are to move this problem from the streets to the courts.

I am also asking Congress to authorize the Federal Government to participate more fully in lawsuits designed to end segregation in public education. We have succeeded in persuading many districts to desegregate voluntarily. Dozens have admitted Negroes without violence. Today a Negro is attending a State-supported institution in every one of our 50 States, but the pace is very slow.

Too many Negro children entering segregated grade schools at the time of the Supreme Court's decision 9 years ago will enter segregated high schools this fall, having suffered a loss which can never be restored. The lack of an adequate education denies the Negro a chance to get a decent job.

The orderly implementation of the Supreme Court decision, therefore, cannot be left solely to those who may not have the economic resources to carry the legal action or who may be subject to harassment.

Other features will be also requested, including greater protection for the right to vote. But legislation, I repeat, cannot solve this problem alone. It must be solved in the homes of every American in every community across our country.

In this respect, I want to pay tribute to those citizens North and South who have been working in their communities to make life better for all. They are acting not out of a sense of legal duty but out of a sense of human decency.

Like our soldiers and sailors in all parts of the world they are meeting freedom's challenge on the firing line, and I salute them for their honor and their courage.

My fellow Americans, this is a problem which faces us all — in every city of the North as well as the South. Today there are Negroes unemployed, two or three times as many compared to whites, inadequate in education, moving into the large cities, unable to find work, young people particularly out of work without hope, denied equal rights, denied the opportunity to eat at a restaurant or lunch counter or go to a movie theater, denied the right to a decent education, denied almost today the right to attend a State university even though qualified. It seems to me that these are matters which concern us all, not merely Presidents or Congressmen or Governors, but every citizen of the United States.

This is one country. It has become one country because all of us and all the people who came here had an equal chance to develop their talents.

We cannot say to 10 percent of the population that you can't have that right; that your children can't have the chance to develop whatever talents they have; that the only way that they are going to get their rights is to go into the streets and demonstrate. I think we owe them and owe ourselves a better country than that.

Therefore, I am asking for your help in making it easier for us to move ahead and to provide the kind of equality of treatment which we would want ourselves; to give a chance for every child to be educated to the limit of his talents.

As I have said before, not every child has an equal talent or an equal ability or an equal motivation, but they should have the equal right to develop their talent and their ability and their motivation, to make something of themselves.

We have a right to expect that the Negro community will be responsible, will uphold the law, but they have a right to expect that the law will be fair, that the Constitution will be color blind, as Justice Harlan said at the turn of the century.

This is what we are talking about and this is a matter which concerns this country and what it stands for, and in meeting it I ask the support of all our citizens.

Thank you very much.

THE NUCLEAR TEST BAN TREATY
July 26, 1963

*On July 25 in Moscow American and Russian negotiaters
signed an agreement to end all atmospheric, underwater,
and outer space testing of nuclear weapons. In the President's words, "a shaft of light had cut into the darkness." Kennedy enumerated the treaty's many advantages and expressed hope that it would be the opening
wedge to future agreements on nuclear weapons.*

I speak to you tonight in a spirit of hope. Eighteen years ago the
advent of nuclear weapons changed the course of the world as well
as the war. Since that time, all mankind has been struggling to escape
from the darkening prospect of mass destruction on earth. In an age
when both sides have come to possess enough nuclear power to destroy
the human race several times over, the world of communism and the
world of free choice have been caught up in a vicious circle of conflicting ideology and interest. Each increase of tension has produced
an increase of arms; each increase of arms has produced an increase
of tension.

In these years, the United States and the Soviet Union have frequently communicated suspicion and warnings to each other, but very
rarely hope. Our representatives have met at the summit and at the
brink; they have met in Washington and in Moscow; in Geneva and at
the United Nations. But too often these meetings have produced only
darkness, discord, or disillusion.

Yesterday a shaft of light cut into the darkness. Negotiations were
concluded in Moscow on a treaty to ban all nuclear tests in the atmosphere, in outer space, and under water. For the first time, an agreement has been reached on bringing the forces of nuclear destruction
under international control — a goal first sought in 1946 when Bernard
Baruch presented a comprehensive control plan to the United Nations.

That plan, and many subsequent disarmament plans, large and
small, have all been blocked by those opposed to international inspection. A ban on nuclear tests, however, requires on-the-spot inspection
only for underground tests. This Nation now possesses a variety of
techniques to detect the nuclear tests of other nations which are conducted in the air or under water, for such tests produce unmistakable
signs which our modern instruments can pick up.

The treaty initialed yesterday, therefore, is a limited treaty which
permits continued underground testing and prohibits only those tests
that we ourselves can police. It requires no control posts, no onsite
inspection, no international body.

We should also understand that it has other limits as well. Any nation which signs the treaty will have an opportunity to withdraw if it finds that extraordinary events related to the subject matter of the treaty have jeopardized its supreme interests; and no nation's right of self-defense will in any way be impaired. Nor does this treaty mean an end to the threat of nuclear war. It will not reduce nuclear stockpiles; it will not halt the production of nuclear weapons; it will not restrict their use in time of war.

Nevertheless, this limited treaty will radically reduce the nuclear testing which would otherwise be conducted on both sides; it will prohibit the United States, the United Kingdom, the Soviet Union, and all others who sign it, from engaging in the atmospheric tests which have so alarmed mankind; and it offers to all the world a welcome sign of hope.

For this is not a unilateral moratorium, but a specific and solemn legal obligation. While it will not prevent this Nation from testing underground, or from being ready to conduct atmospheric tests if the acts of others so require, it gives us a concrete opportunity to extend its coverage to other nations and later to other forms of nuclear tests.

This treaty is in part the product of Western patience and vigilance. We have made clear — most recently in Berlin and Cuba — our deep resolve to protect our security and our freedom against any form of aggression. We have also made clear our steadfast determination to limit the arms race. In three administrations, our soldiers and diplomats have worked together to this end, always supported by Great Britain. Prime Minister Macmillan joined with President Eisenhower in proposing a limited test ban in 1959, and again with me in 1961 and 1962.

But the achievement of this goal is not a victory for one side — it is a victory for mankind. It reflects no concessions either to or by the Soviet Union. It reflects simply our common recognition of the dangers in further testing.

This treaty is not the millennium. It will not resolve all conflicts, or cause the Communists to forego their ambitions, or eliminate the dangers of war. It will not reduce our need for arms or allies or programs of assistance to others. But it is an important first step — a step towards peace — a step towards reason — a step away from war.

Here is what this step can mean to you and to your children and your neighbors:

First, this treaty can be a step towards reduced world tension and broader areas of agreement. The Moscow talks have reached no agreement on any other subject, nor is this treaty conditioned on any other matter. Under Secretary Harriman made it clear that any nonaggression arrangements across the division in Europe would require full con-

If only one thermonuclear bomb were to be dropped on any American, Russian, or any other city, whether it was launched by accident or design by a madman or by an enemy, by a large nation or by a small, from any corner of the world, that one bomb could release more destructive power on the inhabitants of that one helpless city than all the bombs dropped in the Second World War.

Neither the United States nor the Soviet Union nor the United Kingdom nor France can look forward to that day with equanimity. We have a great obligation, all four nuclear powers have a great obligation, to use whatever time remains to prevent the spread of nuclear weapons, to persuade other countries not to test, transfer, acquire, possess, or produce such weapons.

This treaty can be the opening wedge in that campaign. It provides that none of the parties will assist other nations to test in the forbidden environments. It opens the door for further agreements on the control of nuclear weapons, and it is open for all nations to sign, for it is in the interest of all nations, and already we have heard from a number of countries who wish to join with us promptly.

Fourth and finally, this treaty can limit the nuclear arms race in ways which, on balance, will strengthen our Nation's security far more than the continuation of unrestricted testing. For in today's world, a nation's security does not always increase as its arms increase, when its adversary is doing the same, and unlimited competition in the testing and development of new types of destructive nuclear weapons will not make the world safer for either side. Under this limited treaty, on the other hand, the testing of other nations could never be sufficient to offset the ability of our strategic forces to deter or survive a nuclear attack and to penetrate and destroy an aggressor's homeland.

We have, and under this treaty we will continue to have, the nuclear strength that we need. It is true that the Soviets have tested nuclear weapons of a yield higher than that which we thought to be necessary, but the hundred megaton bomb of which they spoke 2 years ago does not and will not change the balance of strategic power. The United States has chosen, deliberately, to concentrate on more mobile and more efficient weapons, with lower but entirely sufficient yield, and our security is, therefore, not impaired by the treaty I am discussing.

It is also true, as Mr. Khrushchev would agree, that nations cannot afford in these matters to rely simply on the good faith of their adversaries. We have not, therefore, overlooked the risk of secret violations. There is a present a possibility that deep in outer space, that hundreds and thousands and millions of miles away from the earth illegal tests might go undetected. But we already have the capability to construct a system of observation that would make such tests almost impossible to conceal, and we can decide at any time whether such a system is needed in the light of the limited risk to us and the limited reward to others of violations attempted at that range. For any tests which might be conducted so far out in space, which cannot be conducted more easily and efficiently and legally underground, would necessarily be of such magnitude that they would be extremely difficult to conceal. We can also employ new devices to check on the testing of smaller weapons in the lower atmosphere. Any violation, moreover, involves, along with the risk of detection, the end of the treaty and the worldwide consequences for the violator.

Secret violations are possible and secret preparations for a sudden withdrawal are possible, and thus our own vigilance and strength must be maintained, as we remain ready to withdraw and to resume all forms of testing, if we must. But it would be a mistake to assume that this treaty will be quickly broken. The gains of illegal testing are obviously slight compared to their cost, and the hazard of discovery, and the nations which have initialed and will sign this treaty prefer it, in my judgment, to unrestricted testing as a matter of their own self-interests for these nations, too, and all nations, have a stake in limiting the arms race, in holding the spread of nuclear weapons, and in breathing air that is not radioactive. While it may be theoretically possible to demonstrate the risks inherent in any treaty, and such risks in this treaty are small, the far greater risks to our security are the risks of unrestricted testing, the risk of a nuclear arms race, the risk of new nuclear powers, nuclear pollution, and nuclear war.

This limited test ban, in our most careful judgment, is safer by far for the United States than an unlimited nuclear arms race. For all these reasons, I am hopeful that this Nation will promptly approve the limited test ban treaty. There will, of course, be debate in the country and in the Senate. The Constitution wisely requires the advice and consent of the Senate to all treaties, and that consultation has already begun. All this is as it should be. A document which may mark an historic and constructive opportunity for the world deserves an historic and constructive debate.

It is my hope that all of you will take part in that debate, for this treaty is for all of us. It is particularly for our children and our grandchildren, and they have no lobby here in Washington. This debate will involve military, scientific, and political experts, but it must be not left to them alone. The right and the responsibility are yours.

If we are to open new doorways to peace, if we are to seize this rare opportunity for progress, if we are to be as bold and farsighted in our control of weapons as we have been in their invention, then let us now show all the world on this side of the wall and the other that a strong America also stands for peace. There is no cause for complacency.

We have learned in times past that the spirit of one moment or place can be gone in the next. We have been disappointed more than once, and we have no illusions now that there are shortcuts on the road to peace. At many points around the globe the Communists are continuing their efforts to exploit weakness and poverty. Their concentration of nuclear and conventional arms must still be deterred.

The familiar contest between choice and coercion, the familiar places of danger and conflict, are all still there, in Cuba, in Southeast Asia, in Berlin, and all around the globe, still requiring all the strength and the vigilance that we can muster. Nothing could more greatly damage our cause than if we and our allies were to believe that peace has already been achieved, and that our strength and unity were no longer required.

But now, for the first time in many years, the path of peace may be open. No one can be certain what the future will bring. No one can say whether the time has come for an easing of the struggle. But history and our own conscience will judge us harsher if we do not now make every effort to test our hopes by action, and this is the place to begin. According to the ancient Chinese proverb, "A journey of a thousand miles must begin with a single step."

My fellow Americans, let us take that first step. Let us, if we can, step back from the shadows of war and seek out the way of peace. And if that journey is a thousand miles, or even more, let history record that we, in this land, at this time, took the first step.

Thank you and good night.

STATEMENT ON THE WAR IN VIETNAM
Television Interview with Walter Cronkite
September 2, 1963

In this interview and the one following, President Kennedy candidly stated his opinions on the growing American involvement in the Vietnam War. Two months after this interview President Diem and his brother were assassinated and a new government came to power.

Mr. Cronkite: Mr. President, the only hot war we've got running at the moment is of course the one in Viet-Nam, and we have our difficulties there, quite obviously.

THE PRESIDENT. I don't think that unless a greater effort is made by the Government to win popular support that the war can be won out there. In the final analysis, it is their war. They are the ones who have to win it or lose it. We can help them, we can give them equipment, we can send our men out there as advisers, but they have to win it, the people of Viet-Nam, against the Communists.

We are prepared to continue to assist them, but I don't think that the war can be won unless the people support the effort and, in my opinion, in the last 2 months, the government has gotten out of touch with the people.

The repressions against the Buddhists, we felt, were very unwise. Now all we can do is to make it very clear that we don't think this is the way to win. It is my hope that this will become increasingly obvious to the government, that they will take steps to try to bring back popular support for this very essential struggle.

Mr. Cronkite: Do you think this government still has time to regain the support of the people?

THE PRESIDENT. I do. With changes in policy and perhaps with personnel I think it can. If it doesn't make those changes, I would think that the chances of winning it would not be very good.

Mr. Cronkite: Hasn't every indication from Saigon been that President Diem has no intention of changing his pattern?

THE PRESIDENT. If he does not change it, of course, that is his decision. He has been there 10 years and, as I say, he has carried this burden when he has been counted out on a number of occasions.

Our best judgment is that he can't be successful on this basis. We hope that he comes to see that, but in the final analysis it is the people and the government itself who have to win or lose this struggle. All we can do is help, and we are making it very clear, but I don't agree with those who say we should withdraw. That would be a great mistake. I know people don't like Americans to be engaged in this kind of an effort. Forty-seven Americans have been killed in combat with the enemy, but this is a very important struggle even though it is far away.

We took all this — made this effort to defend Europe. Now Europe is quite secure. We also have to participate — we may not like it — in the defense of Asia. . . .

STATEMENT ON THE WAR IN VIETNAM
Television Interview with Chet Huntley and David Brinkley
September 9, 1963

Mr. Huntley: Mr. President, in respect to our difficulties in South Viet-Nam, could it be that our Government tends occasionally to get locked into a policy or an attitude and then finds it difficult to alter or shift that policy?

THE PRESIDENT. Yes, that is true. I think in the case of South Viet-Nam we have been dealing with a government which is in control, for 10 years. In addition, we have felt for the last 2 years that the struggle against the Communists was going better. Since June, however, the difficulties with the Buddhists, we have been concerned about a deterioration, particularly in the Saigon area, which hasn't been felt greatly in the outlying areas but may spread. So we are faced with the problem of wanting to protect the area against the Communists. On the other hand, we have to deal with the government there. That produces a kind of ambivalence in our efforts which exposes us to some criticism. We are using our influence to persuade the government there to take those steps which will win back support. That takes some time and we must be patient, we must persist.

Mr. Huntley: Are we likely to reduce our aid to South Viet-Nam now?

THE PRESIDENT. I don't think we think that would be helpful at this time. If you reduce your aid, it is possible you could have some effect upon the government structure there. On the other hand, you might have a situation which could bring about a collapse. Strongly in our mind is what happened in the case of China at the end of World War II, where China was lost, a weak government became increasingly unable to control events. We don't want that.

Mr. Brinkley: Mr. President, have you had any reason to doubt this so-called "domino theory," that if South Viet-Nam falls, the rest of southeast Asia will go behind it?

THE PRESIDENT. No, I believe it. I believe it. I think that the struggle is close enough. China is so large, looms so high just beyond the frontiers, that if South Viet-Nam went, it would not only give them an improved geographic position for a guerrilla assault on Malaya, but would also give the impression that the wave of the future in southeast Asia was China and the Communists. So I believe it...

Mr. Brinkley: With so much of our prestige, money, so on, committed in South Viet-Nam, why can't we exercise a little more influence there, Mr. President?

THE PRESIDENT. We have some influence. We have some influence, and we are attempting to carry it out. . . . We can't make the world over, but we can influence the world. The fact of the matter is that with the assistance of the United States, SEATO, southeast Asia and indeed all of Asia has been maintained independent against a powerful force, the Chinese Communists. What I am concerned about is that Americans will get impatient and say because they don't like the governments in Saigon, that we should withdraw. That only makes it easy for the Communists. I think we should stay. We should use our influence in as effective a way as we can, but we should not withdraw. . . .

ADDRESS AT AMHERST COLLEGE
Dedicating the Robert Frost Library
October 26, 1963

This posthumous tribute to Robert Frost eloquently expressed Kennedy's appreciation of the artist and intellectual. The appreciation was generally reciprocated.

This day devoted to the memory of Robert Frost offers an opportunity for reflection which is prized by politicians as well as by others, and even by poets, for Robert Frost was one of the granite figures of our time in America. He was supremely two things: an artist and an American. A nation reveals itself not only by the men it produces but also by the men it honors, the men it remembers.

In America, our heroes have customarily run to men of large accomplishments. But today this college and country honors a man whose contribution was not to our size but to our spirit, not to our political beliefs but to our insight, not to our self-esteem, but to our self-comprehension. In honoring Robert Frost, we therefore can pay honor to the deepest sources of our national strength. That strength takes many forms, and the most obvious forms are not always the most significant. The men who create power make an indispensable contribution to the Nation's greatness, but the men who question power make a contribution just as indispensable, especially when that questioning is disinterested, for they determine whether we use power or power uses us.

Our national strength matters, but the spirit which informs and controls our strength matters just as much. This was the special significance of Robert Frost. He brought an unsparing instinct for reality to bear on the platitudes and pieties of society. His sense of the human tragedy fortified him against self-deception and easy consolation. "I have been," he wrote, "one acquainted with the night." And because he knew the midnight as well as the high noon, because he understood the ordeal as well as the triumph of the human spirit, he gave his age strength with which to overcome despair. At bottom, he held a deep faith in the spirit of man, and it is hardly an accident that Robert Frost coupled poetry and power, for he saw poetry as the means of saving power from itself. When power leads man towards arrogance, poetry reminds him of the richness and diversity of his existence. When power corrupts, poetry cleanses. For art establishes the basic human truth which must serve as the touchstone of our judgment.

The artist, however faithful to his personal vision of reality, becomes the last champion of the individual mind and sensibility against an intrusive society and an officious state. The great artist is thus a solitary figure. He has, as Frost said, a lover's quarrel with the world. In pursuing his perceptions of reality, he must often sail against the currents of his time. This is not a popular role. If Robert Frost was much honored during his lifetime, it was because a good many preferred to ignore his darker truths. Yet in retrospect, we see how the artist's fidelity has strengthened the fibre of our national life.

If sometimes our great artists have been the most critical of our society, it is because their sensitivity and their concern for justice, which must motivate any true artist, makes him aware that our Nation falls short of its highest potential. I see little of more importance to the future of our country and our civilization than full recognition of the place of the artist.

If art is to nourish the roots of our culture, society must set the artist free to follow his vision wherever it takes him. We must never forget that art is not a form of propaganda; it is a form of truth. And as Mr. MacLeish once remarked of poets, there is nothing worse for our trade than to be in style. In free society art is not a weapon and it does not belong to the sphere of polemics and ideology. Artists are not engineers of the soul. It may be different elsewhere. But democratic society — in it, the highest duty of the writer, the composer, the artist is to remain true to himself and to let the chips fall where they may. In serving his vision of the truth, the artist best serves his nation. And the nation which disdains the mission of art invites the fate of Robert Frost's hired man, the fate of having "nothing to look forward to with hope."

I look forward to a great future for America, a future in which our country will match its military strength with our moral restraint, its wealth with our wisdom, its power with our purpose. I look forward to an America which will not be afraid of grace and beauty, which will protect the beauty of our natural environment, which will preserve the great old American houses and squares and parks of our national past, and which will build handsome and balanced cities for our future.

I look forward to an America which will reward achievement in the arts as we reward achievement in business or statecraft. I look forward to an America which will steadily raise the standards of artistic accomplishment and which will steadily enlarge cultural opportunities for all of our citizens. And I look forward to an America which commands respect throughout the world not only for its strength but for its civilization as well. And I look forward to a world which will be safe not only for democracy and diversity but also for personal distinction.

Robert Frost was often skeptical about projects for human improvement, yet I do not think he would disdain this hope. As he wrote during the uncertain days of the Second War:

Take human nature altogether since time began. . .
And it must be a little more in favor of man,
Say a fraction of one percent at the very least. . .
Our hold on the planet wouldn't have so increased.

Because of Mr. Frost's life and work, because of the life and work
of this college, our hold on this planet has increased.

THE WORK COMPLETED AND THE WORK TO BE DONE
Address to the AFL-CIO Convention
November 15, 1963

*A week before his death in Dallas, the President spoke
to the AFL-CIO convention in New York City. He looked
back at the nearly three years of his term and cited the
advancements that had been made. At the same time he
looked ahead at the challenges and opportunities still
to be faced.*

. . . I am glad to come to this convention, and I think that the AFL-CIO, that this convention, and looking back over the years, over this century, can take pride in the actions it has taken, pride in the stand it has made, pride in the things it has done not only for the American labor movement, but for the United States as a whole. . . .

Three years ago, and one week, by a landslide, the people of the United States elected me to the Presidency of this country, and it is possible that you had something to do with that majority of 112,000 votes. And I think it, therefore, appropriate to say something about what we have done, and even more appropriate to say something about what we must do.

With your help and support, with your concern, we have worked to try to improve the lot of the people of the United States. In the last 3 years abroad we have doubled the number of nuclear weapons in our strategic alert forces. In the last 3 years we have increased by 45 percent the number of combat-ready Army divisions. We have increased by 600 percent the number of our counter-insurgency forces; increased by 175 percent our procurement of airlift aircraft, and doubled our polaris and minuteman program. The United States is stronger today than ever before in our history, and with that strength we work for peace.

Here in the United States we have encouraged the peaceful desegregation of schools in 238 districts, theaters in 144 cities, restaurants in 129 cities, and lunch counters in 100 cities, while at the same time taking Executive action to open doors to our citizens in transportation terminals and polling places, and public and private employment. And finally, we have been working to strengthen the economy of the United States, through the Area Redevelopment Act of '61, through the Public Works Acceleration Act of '62, through the Manpower Development and Training Act of '62.

We have increased industry's ability and desire to hire men through the most extensive and promising trade expansion act in our history, through the most comprehensive housing and urban renewal act of all time, through liberalized depreciation guidelines, and through over $1 billion in loans to small businessmen. We have boosted the purchasing power and relieved the distress of some of those least able to take care of themselves, by increasing the minimum wage to $1.25, which is still much too low, and expanding its coverage by 3-1/2 million, which is still too little; by increasing social security benefits to men and women who can retire at the age of 62; by granting for the first time in the history of the United States public assistance to several hundred thousand children of unemployed fathers; and by extending the benefits of nearly 3 million jobless workers.

By doing these things, and others, we have attempted to work for the benefit of our people. And I can assure you that if we can obtain — and I see no good reason why we should not — if we can obtain the prompt passage of the pending $11 billion tax reduction bill, we will be sailing by next April on the winds of the longest and strongest peacetime expansion in the history of the United States.

Our national output 3 years ago was $500 billion. In January, 3 years later, it will be $600 billion, a record rise of $100 billion in 36 months. For the first time in history we have 70 million men and women at work. For the first time in history factory earnings have exceeded $100 a week, and even the stock market has broken all records, although we only get credit when it goes down. The average factory worker takes home $10 a week more than he did 3 years ago, and 2-1/2 million people more are at work. In fact, if the economy during the last 2-1/2 years had grown at the same lagging pace which it did in the last 2-1/2 years of the fifties, unemployment today would be 8 percent. In short, we have made progress, but all of us know that more progress must be made. That is what we are here about. I am here today to talk about the right to work, the right to have a job in this country in a time of prosperity in the United States. That is the real right to work issue in 1963. In spite of this progress, this country must move so fast to even stand still.

Productivity goes up so fast. The number of people coming into the labor market so increases. Ten million more jobs are needed in the next 2-1/2 years. Even with this astonishing economic progress, which in the last 18 months has meant that the United States has grown faster economically than France and Germany, than any country in Europe but two, even with this extraordinary economic progress in the last 18 months we still have an unemployment rate of 5-1/2 percent, 4 million people out of work. Productivity goes up so fast, so many millions come into the labor market, that unless we have the most extraordinary economic progress in the history of our country we cannot possibly make a dent in the 5-1/2 percent figure.

So while we take some satisfaction in what we have done and tried to do, this group more than any knows how much we still have left to do. . . .

Four million people are out of work. All of the people who opposed the efforts we are making to try to improve the economic climate of the United States, who talked to us so long about socialism and deficits and all the rest, should look at that figure. Four million people out of work. And judging from last summer's statistics, three times that many have experienced some unemployment. And that hanging over the labor market makes it more difficult for those of you who speak for labor at the bargaining table to speak with force. When there are so many people out of work it affects the whole economic climate. That is why I think that this issue of economic security, of jobs, is the basic issue facing the United States in 1963, and I wish we could get everybody talking about it. A quarter of the people we are talking about are out of work 15 weeks or longer and their families feel it.

This is a year of prosperity, of record prosperity — and 1954 was a year of recession — yet our unemployment rate is as high today as it was in 1954. Last year's loss of man-hours in terms of those willing but unable to find full-time work was a staggering one billion workdays lost, equivalent to shutting down the entire country for 3 weeks with no pay. That is an intolerable waste for this rich country of ours.

That is why I say that economic security is the number one issue today. It is not so recognized by everyone. There are those who oppose the tax cut, the youth employment bill, who oppose more money for depressed areas and job retraining, and other public needs. And they are powerful and articulate. They are campaigning on a platform of so-called individual initiative. They talk loudly of deficits and socialism, but they do not have a single constructive job-creating program of their own, and they oppose the efforts that we are making. And I do not believe that selling TVA is a program to put people to work.

There are those who support our efforts for jobs but say it isn't the number one issue. Some may say that civil rights is the number one issue. This Nation needs the passage of our bill, if we are to fulfill our constitutional obligations, but no one gains from a fair employment practice bill if there is no employment to be had; no one gains by being admitted to a lunch counter if he has no money to spend. No one gains from attending a better school if he doesn't have a job after graduation. No one thinks much of the right to own a good home and to sleep in a good hotel or go to the theater if he has no work and no money. The civil rights legislation is important. But to make that legislation effective we need jobs in the United States.

Some may say that the number one domestic issue is education, and this Nation must improve its education. What concerns me almost more than anything is the statistic that there will be 8 million young boys and girls coming into the labor market in the sixties who have not graduated from high school. Where are they going to find jobs? Which of your unions is going to be able to put them to work, 8 million of them? But the best schools, the best teachers, the best books – all these are of no avail if there are no jobs.

The out-of-work college graduate is just as much out of work as a school dropout. The family beset by unemployment cannot send a child to college. It may even encourage him to drop out of high school to find a job which he will not keep. Education is a key to the growth of this country. We must educate our children as our most valuable resource. We must make it possible for those who have talent to go to college, but only if those who are educated can find a job.

If jobs are the most important domestic issue that this country faces, then clearly no single step can now be more important in sustaining the economy of the United States than the passage of our tax bill. Now this will help consumer markets and build investment demand and build business incentives and, therefore, provide jobs for a total addition to the economy of the United States in the next months of nearly $30 billion.

We dare not wait for this tax cut until it is too late, as perhaps some would have. On the average, this Nation's period of peacetime expansion before the downturn comes leading to a recession, on the average it has lasted 28 months since 1920 and 32 months since the end of the Second World War. Today we are already in our 33rd month of economic expansion, and we urgently need that tax cut as insurance against a recession next year. And we need that cut where it will do the most good, and the benefits mostly will go to those 2 or 3 million people who will, out of that bill, find new jobs.

But tax cuts are not enough and jobs are not enough, and higher earnings and greater growth and record prosperity are not enough unless that prosperity is used to sustain a better society. We can take real pride in a $600 billion economy and 70 million jobs only when they are underwriting to the fullest extent possible to improve our schools, to rebuild our cities, to counsel our youth, to assure our health, and to care for our aged and infirm.

Next Monday the House Ways and Means Committee will open its hearings on a bill too long delayed to provide hospital insurance for our older citizens. These hearings are desirable, but the facts are known. Our older and retired workers are sick more often and for longer periods than the rest of the population. Their income is only half of that of our younger citizens. They cannot afford either the rising cost of hospital care or the rising cost of hospital insurance. Their children cannot afford to pay hospital bills for three generations – for their children, for themselves, and for their parents. I have no doubt that most children are willing to try to do it, but they cannot.

And I think that the United States should meet its responsibilities as a proud and resourceful country. I cannot tell whether we are going to get this legislation before Christmas, but I can say that I believe that this Congress will not go home next summer to the people of the United States without passing this bill. I think we should stay there until we do. . . .

The United States is the keystone in the arch of freedom. However disappointing life may be around the workd, the forces of freedom are still in the majority, and they are in the majority after 18 years because the United States has been willing to bear the burden. There are 1 million Americans serving the United States outside its borders. No country in the history of the world has a comparable record. No country has ever sent so many of its sons and daughters around the globe, not to oppress but to help people be free. But we can maintain them, we can maintin our commitments, we can strengthen the cause of freedom, we can provide equality of opportunity for our people only in the final analysis if we provide for a growing and buoyant and progressive economy here in the United States. And that is what we are attempting to do. . . .

Marshal Lyautey, the great French marshal, went out to his gardener and asked him to plant a tree. The gardener said, "Why plant it? It won't flower for 100 years." "In that case," the Marshal said, "plant it this afternoon."

That is what we have to do.

BIBLIOGRAPHICAL AIDS

BIBLIOGRAPHICAL AIDS

Although less than a decade has elapsed since John F. Kennedy's assassination, already a formidable number of books and articles have attempted to assess the man. Unfortunately, but understandably, most of these works will be consigned to oblivion, products of inadequate perspective and insufficient primary sources. A few studies, however, will remain valuable. Most of the latter are by close associates of the President. For the reader who desires a comprehensive listing and evaluation of Kennedy materials as of 1968, he is urged to consult the volume by James T. Crown, The Kennedy Literature, a bibliographical essay on John F. Kennedy New York, 1968.

SOURCE MATERIALS

Until Kennedy's personal papers and those of key members of his administration have been freely opened to scholars, research will necessarily be limited. James Crown, in the bibliographical essay cited above, discusses the Kennedy Library in Cambridge, Massachusetts, and suggests research possibilities within existing limitattions.

Kennedy's public messages and speeches may be followed in a number of sources. For the Presidency, the authoritative source is the Public Papers of the Presidents of the United States, John F. Kennedy. Washington, 1962-64, three large volumes which contain the news conferences in addition to his prepared addresses. Other, shorter collections include:

Chase, Harold W., and Lerman, Allen H., eds. Kennedy and the Press, the News Conferences. New York, 1965. Texts of the news conferences.

Gardner, John W., ed. To Turn the Tide. New York, 1962. Speeches of his first year in the Presidency.

Kraus, Sidney, ed. <u>The Great Debates; Background – Perspective – Effects.</u> Bloomington, Ind., 1960. Texts of the famous Kennedy-Nixon television debates of the 1960 campaign; scholarly and journalistic comments on the effect of the debates on voting patterns supplement the texts.

Nevins, Allan., ed. <u>The Burden and the Glory.</u> New York, 1964. A well-chosen selection of speeches from the second and third years of his Presidency.

————. <u>The Strategy of Peace, Senator John F. Kennedy.</u> New York, 1960. Speeches, mostly on foreign policy, from the mid and late 1950's. Also included is a discussion in December, 1959, between Senator Kennedy and John Fischer, editor of Harper's Magazine.

BOOKS BY KENNEDY

John F. Kennedy, <u>A Nation of Immigrants.</u> New York, 1964. A brief history of United States immigration policies and a plea for a liberalization of those policies.

————. <u>Profiles in Courage.</u> New York, 1956. The Pulitzer Prize winning volume which sketches courageous American politicians in action.

————. <u>Why England Slept.</u> New York, 1940. Kennedy's senior honors' thesis at Harvard, slightly revised, an analysis of England's unpreparedness in the late 1930's.

BIOGRAPHIES AND SPECIAL STUDIES

Bishop, Jim. <u>A Day in the Life of President Kennedy.</u> New York, 1964. An hour-by-hour account of the President at work and with his family.

Burns, James MacGregor. <u>John Kennedy: A Political Profile.</u> New York, 1960. Burns had unrestricted access to Kennedy's personal papers as well as papers of the Kennedy family. He also interviewed the then Senator and his family extensively. The result is a fine book on Kennedy's life and career up to 1960. Burns admires his subject but not uncritically.

Crown, James T. Kennedy in Power. New York, 1961. Details the first year of the Presidency.

Damere, Lee. The Cape Cod Years of John Fitzgerald Kennedy. Englewood Cliffs, New Jersey, 1967. Informative on Kennedy's Hyannis Port Life.

Donald, Aida Dipace, ed. John F. Kennedy and the New Frontier. New York, 1966. An excellent collection of nineteen articles and excerpts from books previously published.

Donovan, Robert J. PT-109: John F. Kennedy in World War II. New York, 1961. Extols Kennedy's courage in the incident that later was made into a movie.

Fay, Paul B., Jr. The Pleasure of his Company. New York, 1966. An anecdotal reminiscense by one who met Kennedy in World War II.

Fuchs, Lawrence H. John F. Kennedy and American Catholicism. New York, 1967. Studies the interaction between politics and Catholicism.

Golden, Harry. Mr. Kennedy and the Negroes. New York, 1964. A view of Southern racism. Kennedy is highly praised for his efforts in civil rights.

Harris, Seymour. Economics of the Kennedy Years, and a Look Ahead New York, 1964. Defends Kennedy's policies.

Heath, James. The Kennedy Administration and the Business Community. Chicago, 1969.

Hillsman, Roger. To Move A Nation: The Politics of Foreign Policy in the Administration of John F. Kennedy. New York, 1967. Hillsman was director of the State Department's Bureau of Intelligence and Research and later served as Assistant Secretary of State for Far Eastern Affairs. His book is part memoir, part history. The chapters on Southeast Asia are especially revealing.

Kennedy, Robert F. Thirteen Days. Philadelphia, 1969. The story of the dramatic and frightening Cuban missile crisis of 1962 by the President's brother and Attorney General.

Lasky, Victor. J.F.K., The Man and the Myth. New York, 1963. A sharp-
    ly critical book. Lasky finds fault with virtually everything
    Kennedy did or proposed.

Lincoln, Evelyn. My Twelve Years With John F. Kennedy. New York,
    1965. Mrs. Lincoln was Kennedy's personal secretary and this
    volume is largely based on her diary.

Manchester, William. Portrait of a President. Boston, 1962. A highly
    admiring portrait.

Salinger, Pierre. With Kennedy. Garden City, N.Y., 1966. Salinger,
    Kennedy's press secretary, discusses the issue of news manage-
    ment.

Schlesinger, Arthur M., Jr. A Thousand Days: John F. Kennedy in the
    White House. Boston, 1965. The most detailed work on Kennedy
    as President. Schlesinger served as a Special Assistant to
    the White House, with particular responsibility for diplomatic
    problems. His discussion of Latin American and Southeast
    Asian affairs is the strongest feature of the book. Schlesinger,
    well known as the historian of the Ages of Jackson and Franklin
    D. Roosevelt, has contributed a brilliantly written interpreta-
    tion and one destined to endure.

Sidey, Hugh. John F. Kennedy, President. New York, 1963. A sympa-
    thetic treatment by a Time magazine reporter.

Sorenson, Theodore C. Decision Making in the White House: the Olive
    Branch or the Arrows. New York, 1963. Sometimes called
    Kennedy's alter ego after having worked for him as a speech
    writer and adviser for ten years, Sorenson here deals with
    the office of the Presidency and not the man.

————. Kennedy. New York. 1965. A lengthy and well-written biogra-
    phy, giving fascinating insights into Kennedy's habits of work
    and his private responses to the crises he faced. Like Schles-
    inger's, this book will continue to remain useful.

Whalen, Richard, J. The Founding Father. New York, 1964. A study
    of the President's influential father, Joseph P. Kennedy.

White, Theodore. The Making of the President, 1960. New York, 1961.
    A superb reporter's absorbing account of the election campaign.

Wicker, Tom. J.F.K. and L.B.J. New York, 1968. A comparison by
    the New York Times' correspondent.

BOOKS ON THE ASSASSINATION

Some of the books in the previous section have brief descriptions of the events of November 22, 1963. More substantial investigations are noted below.

Bishop, Jim. The Day Kennedy Was Shot. New York, 1968. A minute reconstruction of events generally in agreement with the conclusions of the Warren Commission.

Epstein, Edward J. Inquest: The Warren Commission and the Establishment of Truth. New York, 1966. Dispassionate criticism of the Warren Commission's methods; based on interviews with the Commission's aides and attorneys.

Lane, Mark. Rush To Judgment. New York, 1966. Argues that Lee Harvey Oswald's guilt was not established by the Warren Commission "beyond a reasonable doubt."

Manchester, William. The Death of a President; November 20-25, 1963. New York, 1967. A book commissioned by the Kennedy family, its publication stirred up a bitter legal quarrel.

The Warren Commission On The Assassination of President Kennedy New York, 1964. A one volume condensation of the multi-volumed report.

ARTICLES

Carleton, William G. "Kennedy in History: An Early Appraisal," Antioch Review, XXVII (Fall, 1964), 277-99.

Dector, Midge. "Kennedyism," Commentary, XLIX (January, 1970), 19-27.

Eckhardt, William, and White, Ralph K. "A test of the mirror-image hypothesis: Kennedy and Khrushchev," Journal of Conflict Resolution, XI (September, 1967), 325-32.

Kaleb, George. "Kennedy as Statesman," Commentary, XLIV (June, 1966), 54-60.

Neustadt, Richard E. "Kennedy in the Presidency: A Premature Appraisal," Political Science Quarterly, LXXIX (September, 1964), 321-34.

Shannon, William V. "The Kennedy Administration, the Early Months," American Scholar. XLII (Autumn, 1961).

Tugwell, Rexford G. "The President and His Helpers: A Review Article," Political Science Quarterly, LXXXII (June, 1967), 253-67.

THE PRESIDENCY

Bailey, Thomas A. Presidential Greatness: The Image and the Man from George Washington to the Present. New York, 1966. A prominent historian's interpretations written in a lively style. He concludes that Kennedy, had he lived and served two full terms in office, probably would have been ranked by scholars as a "Near Great or even a Great" President. The book is notable for its humorous yet insightful characterizations.

Binkley, Wilfred E. The Man in the White House: His Powers and Duties. New York, 1964. revised edition. A careful overview.

Brown, Stuart Gerry. The American Presidency: Leadership, Partisanship, and Popularity. New York, 1966. A study of the relationship of popularity and partisanship to effective leadership; he concludes that Kennedy might have been more effective had he been more vigorously partisan.

Burns, James MacGregor. Presidential Government: The Crucible of Leadership. New York, 1966. By Kennedy's biographer, this author has written widely and incisively on political theory and practice.

Kane, Joseph Nathan. Facts about the Presidents. New York, 1968. Essential and random data, including important dates, Cabinet members, and a brief biography of each President.

Laski, Harold J. The American Presidency. New York, 1940. A massive analysis by the English scholar.

Neustadt, R. E. Presidential Power. New York, 1960. A key study which emphasizes the modern presidents and by a man to whom Kennedy turned for advice in setting up his government.

Rossiter, Clinton. The American Presidency. New York, 1960. Well regarded essays on such topics as "the powers of the Presidency" and "the limits of the Presidency."

NAME INDEX

THE PRESIDENTIAL CHRONOLOGIES

GEORGE WASHINGTON*
  edited by Howard F. Bremer
JOHN ADAMS*
  edited by Howard F. Bremer
THOMAS JEFFERSON **
  edited by Arthur Bishop
JAMES MADISON**
  edited by Ian Elliot
JAMES MONROE*
  edited by Ian Elliot
JOHN QUINCY ADAMS*
  edited by Kenneth Jones
ANDREW JACKSON**
  edited by Kenneth Jones
MARTIN VAN BUREN**
  edited by Irving J. Sloan
HARRISON/ TYLER***
  edited by David A. Durfee
JAMES K. POLK*
  edited by John J. Farrell
TAYLOR/ FILLMORE**
  edited by John J. Farrell
THEODORE ROOSEVELT**
  edited by Gilbert Black
WILLIAM HOWARD TAFT*
  edited by Gilbert Black
WOODROW WILSON**
  edited by Robert I. Vexler
FRANKLIN PIERCE*
  edited by Irving J. Sloan
JAMES BUCHANAN*
  edited by Irving J. Sloan
ABRAHAM LINCOLN***
  edited by Ian Elliot
ANDREW JOHNSON*
  edited by John N. Dickinson

ULYSSESS S. GRANT**
  edited by Philip R. Moran
RUTHERFORD B. HAYES*
  edited by Arthur Bishop
GARFIELD/ ARTHUR***
  edited by Howard B. Furer
GROVER CLEVELAND**
  edited by Robert I. Vexler
BENJAMIN HARRISON*
  edited by Harry J. Sievers
WILLIAM McKINLEY*
  edited by Harry J. Sievers
WARREN G. HARDING**
  edited by Philip R. Moran
CALVIN COOLIDGE***
  edited by Philip R. Moran
HERBERT HOOVER*
  edited by Arnold Rice
FRANKLIN D. ROOSEVELT****
  edited by Howard F. Bremer
HARRY S TRUMAN***
  edited by Howard B. Furer
DWIGHT D. EISENHOWER***
  edited by Robert I. Vexler
JOHN F. KENNEDY*
  edited by Ralph A. Stone
LYNDON B. JOHNSON***
  edited by Howard B. Furer

*	96 pages,	$3.00
**	128 pages,	$4.00
***	160 pages,	$5.00
****	224 pages,	$7.00